七赤金星命

Seven Red Life Star

Feng Shui Essentials: Xuan Kong Nine Life Star
SEVEN RED LIFE STAR

Copyright © 2011 by Joey Yap
All rights reserved worldwide.
First Edition July 2011

All intellectual property rights contained or in relation to this book belongs to Joey Yap.

No part of this book may be copied, used, subsumed, or exploited in fact, field of thought or general idea, by any other authors or persons, or be stored in a retrieval system, transmitted or reproduced in any way, including but not limited to digital copying and printing in any form whatsoever worldwide without the prior agreement and written permission of the author.

The author can be reached at:

Mastery Academy of Chinese Metaphysics Sdn. Bhd. (611143-A)
19-3, The Boulevard, Mid Valley City,
59200 Kuala Lumpur, Malaysia.
Tel   : +603-2284 8080
Fax   : +603-2284 1218
Website : www.masteryacademy.com

DISCLAIMER:

The author, Joey Yap and the publisher, JY Books Sdn Bhd, have made their best efforts to produce this high quality, informative and helpful book. They have verified the technical accuracy of the information and contents of this book. Any information pertaining to the events, occurrences, dates and other details relating to the person or persons, dead or alive, and to the companies have been verified to the best of their abilities based on information obtained or extracted from various websites, newspaper clippings and other public media. However, they make no representation or warranties of any kind with regard to the contents of this book and accept no liability of any kind for any losses or damages caused or alleged to be caused directly or indirectly from using the information contained herein.

Published by JY Books Sdn. Bhd. (659134-T)

Table of content :

1	LIFE STAR REFERENCE TABLE	7
2	INTRODUCTION	12
3	**YOUR XUAN KONG LIFE STAR**	23
	Basic Attributes	24
4	**YOUR FENG SHUI ESSENTIALS**	27
	Directions	29
	Taking the Direction using a Compass	33
	Favorable Directions	39
	Unfavorable Directions	49
	Bed Alignment Direction	58
	Best Floor	60
	Personal Grand Duke Direction	65
	Personal Clash Direction	71
	Flying Star Effects	76
5	**THE FIVE ELEMENT**	97

6	**CHARACTERISTICS OF STAR**	109
	The Good	111
	The Bad	117
7	**CAREER AND WEALTH**	123
	Characteristics at work	124
	Suitable Job Roles	128
	Career and Wealth Guide	132
8	**RELATIONSHIPS**	139
	Guide for Relationships	140
9	**HEALTH**	145
	Guide for Health	146
10	**COMPATIBILITY with OTHER LIFE STARS**	151

LIFE STAR REFERENCE TABLE

Year Pillar and Gua Number Reference Table for 1912 - 2055

Animal	Year of Birth			Gua Number for Male	Gua Number for Female	Year of Birth			Gua Number for Male	Gua Number for Female
Rat	1912	壬子 Ren Zi	Water Rat	7	8	1936	丙子 Bing Zi	Fire Rat	1	5
Ox	1913	癸丑 Gui Chou	Water Ox	6	9	1937	丁丑 Ding Chou	Fire Ox	9	6
Tiger	1914	甲寅 Jia Yin	Wood Tiger	5	1	1938	戊寅 Wu Yin	Earth Tiger	8	7
Rabbit	1915	乙卯 Yi Mao	Wood Rabbit	4	2	1939	己卯 Ji Mao	Earth Rabbit	7	8
Dragon	1916	丙辰 Bing Chen	Fire Dragon	3	3	1940	庚辰 Geng Chen	Metal Dragon	6	9
Snake	1917	丁巳 Ding Si	Fire Snake	2	4	1941	辛巳 Xin Si	Metal Snake	5	1
Horse	1918	戊午 Wu Wu	Earth Horse	1	5	1942	壬午 Ren Wu	Water Horse	4	2
Goat	1919	己未 Ji Wei	Earth Goat	9	6	1943	癸未 Gui Wei	Water Goat	3	3
Monkey	1920	庚申 Geng Shen	Metal Monkey	8	7	1944	甲申 Jia Shen	Wood Monkey	2	4
Rooster	1921	辛酉 Xin You	Metal Rooster	7	8	1945	乙酉 Yi You	Wood Rooster	1	5
Dog	1922	壬戌 Ren Xu	Water Dog	6	9	1946	丙戌 Bing Xu	Fire Dog	9	6
Pig	1923	癸亥 Gui Hai	Water Pig	5	1	1947	丁亥 Ding Hai	Fire Pig	8	7
Rat	1924	甲子 Jia Zi	Wood Rat	4	2	1948	戊子 Wu Zi	Earth Rat	7	8
Ox	1925	乙丑 Yi Zi	Wood Ox	3	3	1949	己丑 Ji Chou	Earth Ox	6	9
Tiger	1926	丙寅 Bing Yin	Fire Tiger	2	4	1950	庚寅 Geng Yin	Metal Tiger	5	1
Rabbit	1927	丁卯 Ding Mao	Fire Rabbit	1	5	1951	辛卯 Xin Mao	Metal Rabbit	4	2
Dragon	1928	戊辰 Wu Chen	Earth Dragon	9	6	1952	壬辰 Ren Chen	Water Dragon	3	3
Snake	1929	己巳 Ji Si	Earth Snake	8	7	1953	癸巳 Gui Si	Water Snake	2	4
Horse	1930	庚午 Geng Wu	Metal Horse	7	8	1954	甲午 Jia Wu	Wood Horse	1	5
Goat	1931	辛未 Xin Wei	Metal Goat	6	9	1955	乙未 Yi Wei	Wood Goat	9	6
Monkey	1932	壬申 Ren Shen	Water Monkey	5	1	1956	丙申 Bing Shen	Fire Monkey	8	7
Rooster	1933	癸酉 Gui You	Water Rooster	4	2	1957	丁酉 Ding You	Fire Rooster	7	8
Dog	1934	甲戌 Jia Xu	Wood Dog	3	3	1958	戊戌 Wu Xu	Earth Dog	6	9
Pig	1935	乙亥 Yi Hai	Wood Pig	2	4	1959	己亥 Ji Hai	Earth Pig	5	1

- Please note that the date for the Chinese Solar Year starts on Feb 4. This means that if you were born in Feb 2 of 2002, you belong to the previous year 2001.

Year Pillar and Gua Number Reference Table for 1912 - 2055

Animal	Year of Birth			Gua Number for Male	Gua Number for Female	Year of Birth			Gua Number for Male	Gua Number for Female
Rat	1960	庚子 Geng Zi	Metal Rat	4	2	1984	甲子 Jia Zi	Wood Rat	7	8
Ox	1961	辛丑 Xin Chou	Metal Ox	3	3	1985	乙丑 Yi Chou	Wood Ox	6	9
Tiger	1962	壬寅 Ren Yin	Water Tiger	2	4	1986	丙寅 Bing Yin	Fire Tiger	5	1
Rabbit	1963	癸卯 Gui Mao	Water Rabbit	1	5	1987	丁卯 Ding Mao	Fire Rabbit	4	2
Dragon	1964	甲辰 Jia Chen	Wood Dragon	9	6	1988	戊辰 Wu Chen	Earth Dragon	3	3
Snake	1965	乙巳 Yi Si	Wood Snake	8	7	1989	己巳 Ji Si	Earth Snake	2	4
Horse	1966	丙午 Bing Wu	Fire Horse	7	8	1990	庚午 Geng Wu	Metal Horse	1	5
Goat	1967	丁未 Ding Wei	Fire Goat	6	9	1991	辛未 Xin Wei	Metal Goat	9	6
Monkey	1968	戊申 Wu Shen	Earth Monkey	5	1	1992	壬申 Ren Shen	Water Monkey	8	7
Rooster	1969	己酉 Ji You	Earth Rooster	4	2	1993	癸酉 Gui You	Water Rooster	7	8
Dog	1970	庚戌 Geng Xu	Metal Dog	3	3	1994	甲戌 Jia Xu	Wood Dog	6	9
Pig	1971	辛亥 Xin Hai	Metal Pig	2	4	1995	乙亥 Yi Hai	Wood Pig	5	1
Rat	1972	壬子 Ren Zi	Water Rat	1	5	1996	丙子 Bing Zi	Fire Rat	4	2
Ox	1973	癸丑 Gui Chou	Water Ox	9	6	1997	丁丑 Ding Chou	Fire Ox	3	3
Tiger	1974	甲寅 Jia Yin	Wood Tiger	8	7	1998	戊寅 Wu Yin	Earth Tiger	2	4
Rabbit	1975	乙卯 Yi Mao	Wood Rabbit	7	8	1999	己卯 Ji Mao	Earth Rabbit	1	5
Dragon	1976	丙辰 Bing Chen	Fire Dragon	6	9	2000	庚辰 Geng Chen	Metal Dragon	9	6
Snake	1977	丁巳 Ding Si	Fire Snake	5	1	2001	辛巳 Xin Si	Metal Snake	8	7
Horse	1978	戊午 Wu Wu	Earth Horse	4	2	2002	壬午 Ren Wu	Water Horse	7	8
Goat	1979	己未 Ji Wei	Earth Goat	3	3	2003	癸未 Gui Wei	Water Goat	6	9
Monkey	1980	庚申 Geng Shen	Metal Monkey	2	4	2004	甲申 Jia Shen	Wood Monkey	5	1
Rooster	1981	辛酉 Xin You	Metal Rooster	1	5	2005	乙酉 Yi You	Wood Rooster	4	2
Dog	1982	壬戌 Ren Xu	Water Dog	9	6	2006	丙戌 Bing Xu	Fire Dog	3	3
Pig	1983	癸亥 Gui Hai	Water Pig	8	7	2007	丁亥 Ding Hai	Fire Pig	2	4

- Please note that the date for the Chinese Solar Year starts on Feb 4. This means that if you were born in Feb 2 of 2002, you belong to the previous year 2001.

Year Pillar and Gua Number Reference Table for 1912 - 2055

Animal	Year of Birth			Gua Number for		Year of Birth			Gua Number for	
				Male	Female				Male	Female
Rat	2008	戊子 Wu Zi	Earth Rat	1	5	2032	壬子 Ren Zi	Water Rat	4	2
Ox	2009	己丑 Ji Chou	Earth Ox	9	6	2033	癸丑 Gui Chou	Water Ox	3	3
Tiger	2010	庚寅 Geng Yin	Metal Tiger	8	7	2034	甲寅 Jia Yin	Wood Tiger	2	4
Rabbit	2011	辛卯 Xin Mao	Metal Rabbit	7	8	2035	乙卯 Yi Mao	Wood Rabbit	1	5
Dragon	2012	壬辰 Ren Chen	Water Dragon	6	9	2036	丙辰 Bing Chen	Fire Dragon	9	6
Snake	2013	癸巳 Gui Si	Water Snake	5	1	2037	丁巳 Ding Si	Fire Snake	8	7
Horse	2014	甲午 Jia Wu	Wood Horse	4	2	2038	戊午 Wu Wu	Earth Horse	7	8
Goat	2015	乙未 Yi Wei	Wood Goat	3	3	2039	己未 Ji Wei	Earth Goat	6	9
Monkey	2016	丙申 Bing Shen	Fire Monkey	2	4	2040	庚申 Geng Shen	Metal Monkey	5	1
Rooster	2017	丁酉 Ding You	Fire Rooster	1	5	2041	辛酉 Xin You	Metal Rooster	4	2
Dog	2018	戊戌 Wu Xu	Earth Dog	9	6	2042	壬戌 Ren Xu	Water Dog	3	3
Pig	2019	己亥 Ji Hai	Earth Pig	8	7	2043	癸亥 Gui Hai	Water Pig	2	4
Rat	2020	庚子 Geng Zi	Metal Rat	7	8	2044	甲子 Jia Zi	Wood Rat	1	5
Ox	2021	辛丑 Xin Chou	Metal Ox	6	9	2045	乙丑 Yi Chou	Wood Ox	9	6
Tiger	2022	壬寅 Ren Yin	Water Tiger	5	1	2046	丙寅 Bing Yin	Fire Tiger	8	7
Rabbit	2023	癸卯 Gui Mao	Water Rabbit	4	2	2047	丁卯 Ding Mao	Fire Rabbit	7	8
Dragon	2024	甲辰 Jia Chen	Wood Dragon	3	3	2048	戊辰 Wu Chen	Earth Dragon	6	9
Snake	2025	乙巳 Yi Si	Wood Snake	2	4	2049	己巳 Ji Si	Earth Snake	5	1
Horse	2026	丙午 Bing Wu	Fire Horse	1	5	2050	庚午 Geng Wu	Metal Horse	4	2
Goat	2027	丁未 Ding Wei	Fire Goat	9	6	2051	辛未 Xin Wei	Metal Goat	3	3
Monkey	2028	戊申 Wu Shen	Earth Monkey	8	7	2052	壬申 Ren Shen	Water Monkey	2	4
Rooster	2029	己酉 Ji You	Earth Rooster	7	8	2053	癸酉 Gui You	Water Rooster	1	5
Dog	2030	庚戌 Geng Xu	Metal Dog	6	9	2054	甲戌 Jia Xu	Wood Dog	9	6
Pig	2031	辛亥 Xin Hai	Metal Pig	5	1	2055	乙亥 Yi Hai	Wood Pig	8	7

- Please note that the date for the Chinese Solar Year starts on Feb 4. This means that if you were born in Feb 2 of 2002, you belong to the previous year 2001.

To download your Seven Red Life Star Reference Chart FREE go to

www.masteryacademy.com/regbook

Here is your unique code for access:

GBSN6017

Introduction

When all is said and done, Feng Shui is the study of how environments affect the people living within them. It can yield advice on which environments, at both a macro and micro level, are 'good' places or 'bad' places to live for given people at given times.

Xuan Kong is only one subsection of the study of Feng Shui and the Life Stars are only one component in the Xuan Kong Feng Shui system. This means that the study of Life Stars gives us only one piece of the overall Feng Shui puzzle but it is an important one!

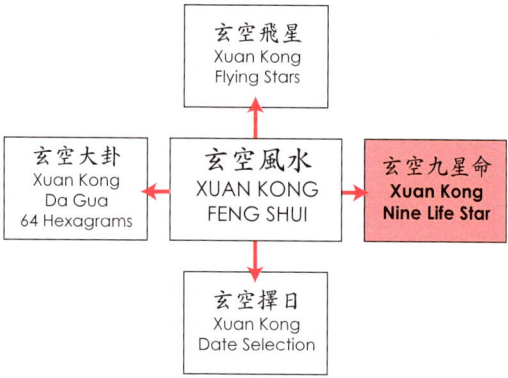

We can use the Xuan Kong Life Star system to help us with a number of practical Feng Shui and interpersonal decisions that make a big impact.

When we assess Feng Shui, we assess four factors: Environment, Buildings, Time and People. This book has been written to complement a number of other Feng Shui titles;

1. *Feng Shui for Homebuyers – Exterior;*
2. *Feng Shui for Homebuyers – Interior;*
3. *Feng Shui for Apartment Buyers;* and
4. *Pure Feng Shui.*

These other books talk about the influence of Environment, Buildings and Time on Feng Shui. This book looks at the final aspect: **People.**

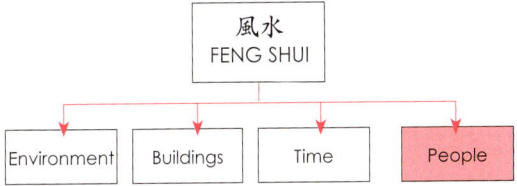

Different people will be affected in different ways by any given environment. The Life Stars directly determine what role the environment plays in the lives of its occupants. Every person is governed by one of the 9 Life Stars. These Stars also help determine key personal characteristics.

In this book, you will learn how the annually changing Xuan Kong Flying Stars interact with your Life Star so that you know what different sectors of your home will bring you. You can then use this information for your own benefit and safety. For maximum benefit, people should seek to align themselves with the direction in their home that yields positive effects. For instance, the #9 Purple Flying Star brings about the potential of career advancement for Star 1 people. Clearly this is a benefit that professionally minded people would like to take advantage of, so they may wish to spend more time absorbing the influence of the #9 Purple Flying Star in their home or place of work. The same Flying Star also indicates a heightened risk of miscarriage for pregnant women though and so pregnant Life Star 1 women should be exercise heightened caution in the presence of this Flying Star, and avoid its influence if possible.

Because the advice generated by this book on Xuan Kong Life Stars takes into account your Life Star when discussing the effects of the Flying Stars, the advice given is highly tailored to your life.

The Positive Side Of You

Your Life Star brings a force to bear on you, wherever you are. This force can have positive or negative effects, depending on the Feng Shui of the environment you reside in.

We are all multi faceted and complex. We have good habits and bad habits; a strong side and a weak side. By correctly tapping into the right Qi your best side will manifest itself more. When you put your best foot forward more in life, more opportunities

and success comes your way. Conversely, if you find yourself under the negative influence of your Life Star, more of your negative personality traits will prevail. Your environment filters out the good or the bad influence of your Life Star. Xuan Kong Feng Shui shows us how we can align ourself to receive the best possible influence. By simply aligning your bed and study desk to correspond with your favourable Personal Directions for example, you can already take one big step towards absorbing the beneficial influence of your Life Star, even whilst you sleep and study! If you are choosing a new home then choosing the correct floor at the correct time will bring further benefits. Avoiding your Personal Grand Duke and Crash Sectors will keep health problems and conflict at bay.

Does all of this mean you must tip-toe around certain rooms in your house or seal them off? No. Feng Shui does not need to become all consuming. If you can easily align your bed so that you receive benefits then why not do so? There are real world limits to what can be done, it is not practical, for instance, to rebuild your home if it does not perfectly cater to the instructions that this book gives. Your ideal floor choice in a condominium may not be available. The list of real world complications goes on.

You can tailor Feng Shui to work for you; making smaller, simple changes so that you reap the maximum possible benefit. The pursuit of good Feng Shui is not intended to take up all of your time and this flexible book is perfect for anyone, no matter how busy or restricted you are in your decisions.

Your Life Star

Everyone falls under the jurisdiction of one of the 9 Life Stars and this will have different consequences for everyone. Your Life Star describes your key skills, characteristics and traits. Some people are creative but reserved, some people are aggressive and driven. What self destructive traits do you have? Do you have a bloated sense of pride or are you prone to gossip? Your Life Star can shine some light on the complexity of your personality and your good and bad traits.

Study of the Life Stars has practical benefits for everyone; it gives you valuable information about others in addition to yourself. Different Life Stars bestow different abilities on people which means that people belonging to each Star will exhibit different characteristics at work. A Star 1 person is diplomatic so they are best suited to roles demanding diplomacy, for example. Accordingly, employers can study the Xuan Kong Life Stars when making work place decisions whilst employees can use the system to help them go about working productively with their colleagues and superiors, even when disagreements arise.

If you become aware of your own harmful tendencies then you can learn to minimize them so you can advance. Similar benefits can be seen in romantic relationships and friendships. Learning that a Star 7 individual needs their space and independence

might help you accommodate this in your dealings with them when you might otherwise have been tempted to be clingy and dependant.

When we understand more about ourselves we can stop ourselves from making mistakes and perhaps forgive certain behaviour in others once we understand where it comes from.

Compatibility Guide

Certain people are, of course, more compatible with each other than others. In partnerships or relationships this takes on a new level of importance. Different Life Stars bestow the qualities of different elements on different people; for example, a Star 1 person has the qualities of water whilst a Star 7 person has the qualities of the Yin Metal element. Just as the elements control, pacify and weaken one another, individuals of the different Stars may dominate, clash with or enrich one another. This book includes a write up of how compatible different Stars are with one another. You may find that a relationship as a Star 1 person with a Star 5 person simply isn't worth the effort. A compatibility guide on each interaction gives you tips on how to best deal with the other Stars for mutual benefit, even taking into account your differences.

Compatible With BaZi Profiling Systems

If you are familiar with the **BaZi Profiling System** then you will be aware that, at first glance, it seems to deal with very similar issues. It can tell us about other preferences and internal view of the world. Do we have an optimistic view of things? Do we blame ourselves too much?

While there is some overlap between the jurisdiction of the Xuan Kong Life Star system and BaZi Profiling System, they are two different systems. They both deal with individual people and their personalities but they are not mutually exclusive. In fact, when studied together, they can be thought of as two pieces of the same puzzle.

The BaZi Profiling System tells us about ourselves and about others. It even tells us things that cannot be observed about others (things people do not communicate). What it can't tell us is how the outside environment plays into the picture. The Xuan Kong Nine Stars help determine *which* qualities are brought out and by what features and external forms in the environment.

Once we know what directions are conducive to good Qi, how external forms (pylons etc) can compound problems related to sectors in the home, which areas of our environment increase the risk of which ailments or even which people can create problems in our lives (compatibility guide) then we can begin shaping our external environment to whatever degree necessary in order to enjoy the most happiness, wealth and success. Xuan

Kong Feng Shui tells you precisely what effect the environment and compass directions will have on which people.

If you are simply interested in learning what makes a person tick rather than making decisions about an ideal environment for them to thrive in then I recommend you take up further study of the BaZi Profiling System. The goal of BaZi is to pinpoint personal deficiencies so that they may be overcome or to highlight personal strengths so that they may be capitalised on.

If you are trying to configure your environment in order to maximize the benefits that your home or place of work bestow upon you in terms of health, wealth and relationships, then the Feng Shui Xuan Kong Life Star system is the one for you.

When you combine the two systems and employ them on yourself you will be able to make the most of your best qualities and then seek out an environment which lets you shine and gives the least resistance. A powerful combination of self improvement and informed decision making!

An Easier Life

Life doesn't have to be difficult. It is possible to effectively dodge conflict, problem situations and health problems if you know they are coming. The Life Stars hold the key to many of the "surprises" that life has in store for us and we can learn to shape our environment to our own advantage. This is exciting stuff! Seeking out the best romantic relationships and business opportunities is a top priority for most people and the power of your Life Star can be called upon in these pursuits.

Even though much is made of the layout of the home with relation to Feng Shui, you won't need to bend over backwards to accommodate the advice given in this book. For instance, where you cannot choose the ideal living floor specified, second and third choices are mentioned. You can take as much or as little from this book as you need without fear of it making you paranoid and prey to "paralysis by analysis". Looking back on your own life, you can most probably think of two or three big mistakes – a bad business deal or choice in romantic partner, perhaps. Avoiding pitfalls of this magnitude in the future is made a whole lot easier when you have some idea of how likely they are to occur. If you can make changes to your environment to further reduce this likelihood then all the better!

I hope that this book expands your world view. Once you know how to utilize them, the Nine Stars can be the harbinger of great fortune instead of misery for you. If you can stay on the 'correct side' of your Star and always position yourself to bask in its positive influence then many happy successes await you.

Joey Yap
July, 2011

 www.facebook.com/joeyyapFB

Author's personal website :
www.joeyyap.com

Academy websites :
www.masteryacademy.com | www.maelearning.com | www.baziprofiling.com

七赤金星命

Seven Red Life Star

Life Star 7	Born in
Male	1921, 1930, 1939, 1948, 1957 1966, 1975, 1984, 1993, 2002
Female	1929, 1938, 1947, 1956, 1965 1974, 1983, 1992, 2001, 2010

- Please note that the date for the Chinese Solar Year starts on Feb 4. This means that if you were born in Feb 2 of 2002, you belong to the previous year 2001.

Your Xuan Kong Life Star

Your Xuan Kong Life Star is Gua #7, and your trigram is called Dui. It looks like this:

For the rest of this book, we will refer to your Gua #7 as Life Star 7.

Basic Attributes of Star 7

Your Life Star 7 is of the Yin Metal element, and as such it shares some of the traits of Metal when it its Yin qualities manifest themselves. Yin Metal is associated with precious metals such as gold, the kind that is used to make fine jewellery. The shape associated with you is the circle, and in classical Chinese Feng Shui the Star 7 is associated with a personable and loquacious young person.

As a Life Star 7, you possesses a silver tongue and the gift of gab! You know just what to say in every situation and rarely find yourself tongue tied. Indeed, you tend to have a cheery disposition and a good taste or extravagance and fun. Luxury is something you covet and you are at your happiest when you feel like you are living the good life. Much of what you do revolves around the pursuit of the finer things in life. You are fast-witted and responsive and easily engage others in conversation and create banter because you're naturally quite sociable.

There is another side to this coin. The Star 7 character has an unhealthy ego and you are prone to indulging your egotistical tendencies. You are a little too smug and

complacent about what you have coming to you. You can be stubborn or childish when things don't suit you and you have a stormy temperament, expecting everyone else to adjust their emotional barometers to benefit you. As a result of this, you can also be prone to arrogance and you find yourself being condescending towards people whom you consider less impressive. Being too invested in earning 'attention' can make you spoiled in the long run, and you can be quite calculating in your efforts to gain attention and be the center of things.

Basic Emotions & Temperament

Plus : Easy-going, joyful, organized, energetic, resourceful

Minus: Stubborn, extravagant, calculating, self-centred, haughty

方向

YOUR FENG SHUI ESSENTIALS

The Feng Shui Essentials comprise Feng Shui Directions, the effects of the Xuan Kong Nine Stars in various sectors and areas of your home and workspace, and the Five Elements.

Each of these factors interact with your Life Star in different ways that will affect how your Life Star manifests itself and determine whether or not it brings out good or bad qualities in you.

Directions

Directions

Direction is an integral component of understanding Xuan Kong Nine Life Stars. Different directions in your home and your place of work can either accentuate or depreciate the strength of your Life Star.

Favorable Direction will highlight or enhance the positive traits of your Life Star, while an Unfavorable Direction will diminish or weaken your Life Star and bring out some of its negative attributes.

The Life Star numbers are categorized into two groups: the East Group and the West Group. The names 'East Group' and 'West Group' are just to demarcate the Greater and Lesser Yin transformation of the Tai Ji. They do not literally represent directions.

East Group Life Stars include 1, 3, 4 and 9. Those who are Life Stars 2, 6, 7 and 8 belong to the West Group. The following table will give you a quick reference of the Auspicious and Inauspicious compass directions of the East and West Group.

East Group 東命

卦 Gua	生氣 Shen Qi Life Generating	天醫 Tian Yi Heavenly Doctor	延年 Yan Nian Longevity	伏位 Fu Wei Stability	禍害 Huo Hai Mishaps	五鬼 Wu Gui Five Ghosts	六煞 Liu Sha Six Killings	絕命 Jue Ming Life Threatening
坎 Kan 1 Water	東南 South East	東 East	南 South	北 North	西 West	東北 North East	西北 North West	西南 South West
震 Zhen 3 Wood	南 South	北 North	東南 South East	東 East	西南 South West	西北 North West	東北 North East	西 West
巽 Xun 4 Wood	北 North	南 South	東 East	東南 South East	西北 North West	西南 South West	西 West	東北 North East
離 Li 9 Fire	東 East	東南 South East	北 North	南 South	東北 North East	西 West	西南 South West	西北 North West

West Group 西命

卦 Gua	生氣 Shen Qi Life Generating	天醫 Tian Yi Heavenly Doctor	延年 Yan Nian Longevity	伏位 Fu Wei Stability	禍害 Huo Hai Mishaps	五鬼 Wu Gui Five Ghosts	六煞 Liu Sha Six Killings	絕命 Jue Ming Life Threatening
坤 Kun 2 Earth	東北 North East	西 West	西北 North West	西南 South West	東 East	東南 South East	南 South	北 North
乾 Qian 6 Metal	西 West	東北 North East	西南 South West	西北 North West	東南 South East	東 East	北 North	南 South
▶ 兌 Dui 7 Metal	西北 North West	西南 South West	東北 North East	西 West	北 North	南 South	東南 South East	東 East
艮 Gen 8 Earth	西南 South West	西北 North West	西 West	東北 North East	南 South	北 North	東 East	東南 South East

The concepts of Favorable and Unfavorable are derived from the Eight Wandering Stars system of the Ba Zhai Eight Mansion Feng Shui 八宅風水.

Each of the 8 directions is governed by a Star. These Wandering Stars will affect each Xuan Kong Life Star in different ways. Each Life Star has four Favorable Directions governed by Auspicious Stars: Sheng Qi 生氣 (Life Generating), Tian Yi 天醫 (Heavenly Doctor), Yan Nian 延年 (Longevity), and Fu Wei 伏位 (Stability).

The four Unfavorable Directions are governed by Inauspicious Stars and include Huo Hai 禍害 (Mishaps), Wu Gui 五鬼 (Five Ghost), Liu Sha 六煞 (Six Killings) and Jue Ming 絕命 (Life Diminishing).

The following diagram shows you the Favorable and Unfavorable Directions for Star 7.

Taking the Direction using a Compass

You will need a compass – or alternatively, the Joey Yap iLuoPan app for iPhone available at the Apple App Store – to determine the direction of your Main Door, Bed and Stove. Hold your compass or iLuoPan at waist level as shown on the illustration below. Your compass or iLuoPan will align to the magnetic North on its own. All you need to know is how to take your direction as indicated on the following pages.

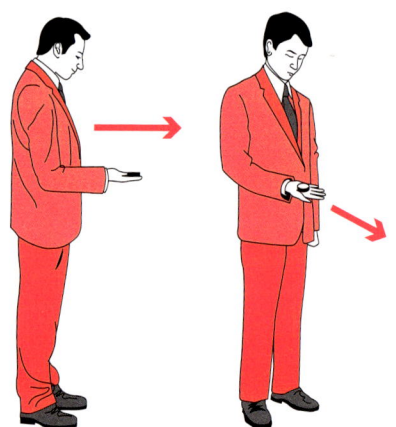

Facing Direction of the Main Door

1. Stand about one foot outside the door looking outwards.

2. Use the square base of your compass to help you align yourself parallel to the door.

3. Read the facing direction on your compass.

Facing Direction of the Bed

1. Measure from the head of the bed where your head is placed when you lie down (the direction the headboard faces) and not the direction your feet face.

Facing Direction of the Stove

1. For modern (gas or electric) stoves, look at the where direction of the cooking knobs (fire igniters) are pointing to determine its facing direction.

2. For traditional stoves that require wood and fire to work, look for their 'fire mouth' as the facing direction.

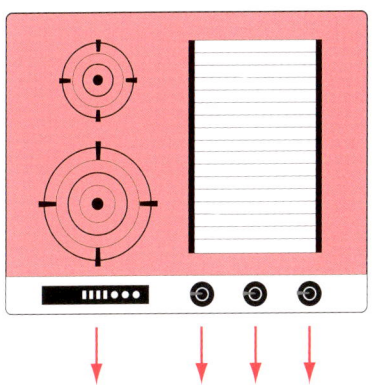

Favorable Directions

Northwest
西北 (307.6°-322.5°)

Life Generating
生氣 *(Sheng Qi)*

 **The basic characteristics of the Sheng Qi Star:**

It brings about promotions, career advancements, strong money and wealth luck, potential political power and authority, and all-round success.

The Sheng Qi Star represents life-generating Qi or energy. It also represents the Wood Element, and hence, governs the facets of success, authority, nobility, status and wealth in life. Wood relates to growth and advancement in life, and as such is an extremely auspicious Star to tap into. For you, the Northwest direction taps into the Sheng Qi potential.

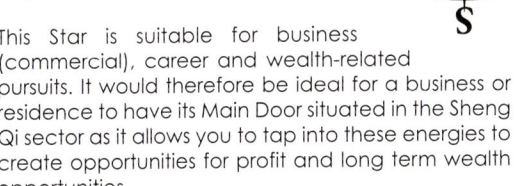

This Star is suitable for business (commercial), career and wealth-related pursuits. It would therefore be ideal for a business or residence to have its Main Door situated in the Sheng Qi sector as it allows you to tap into these energies to create opportunities for profit and long term wealth opportunities.

Sheng Qi is an active star by nature and thus, it is not conducive for rest or sleep-related activities. It is best to avoid having the bed or bedroom located in this sector or for anyone to sleep facing this direction. Use this sector for your work or for active pursuits instead of relaxing ones.

If this sector is missing from a house or is lacking in the office or the premises of a business, the wealth-related aspects of your career or venture will be considerably weakened and it will be a difficult struggle to amass wealth and prosperity.

Southwest
西南 (217.6°-232.5°)

Heavenly Doctor
天醫 (Tian Yi)

 The basic characteristics of the Tian Yi Star:

It brings about general good luck and well-being, as well as positive mentor luck or the presence of sound advisors and guidance.

This Star represents the Earth Element and is therefore the determinant of noble people (mentors) and people of caliber and status. It also denotes your health prospects and physical wellbeing. As such, the Tian Yi Star is best utilized to help generate guidance for your career or for any project which you've embarked upon. It will bring about the help and assistance of others.

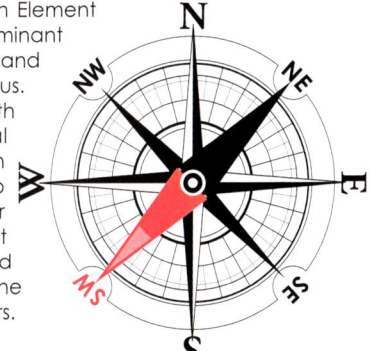

It is also a useful Star for health purposes, and its benefits can be employed when you need to recuperate, recover, or heal from an illness, surgical procedure or health issue.

When the Tian Yin sector is missing from a home or office, your health is likely to suffer because of it. In addition, you will also find help from noble people hard to come by, especially in times of need in life and career matters. You will come across more obstacles and obstructions which you must overcome on your own without the external help of others.

Since the Tian Yi Star represents nobility, it also governs your reputation, respectability, and your oratory powers. It thus has influence on your powers of speech and persuasion, and has some bearing on how you are perceived by others and how well they respond to your verbal overtures.

Northeast
東北 (37.6°-52.5°)

Longevity
延年 *(Yan Nian)*

The basic characteristics of the Yan Nian Star:

It prolongs and enhances life and improves the quality of your life. It promotes good communication with others which in turn makes for good relationships.

The Yan Nian Star represents the Metal Element, and as such governs speech and the effectiveness of your words. If you are looking to establish good relationships and rapport with others, you will need the help of this Star, since it governs aspects of successful networking, communication and relationship building.

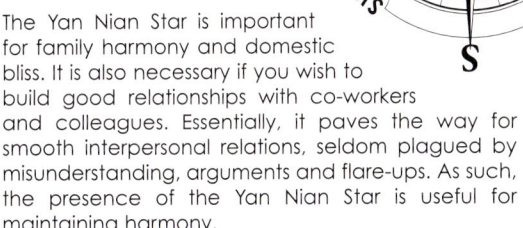

The Yan Nian Star is important for family harmony and domestic bliss. It is also necessary if you wish to build good relationships with co-workers and colleagues. Essentially, it paves the way for smooth interpersonal relations, seldom plagued by misunderstanding, arguments and flare-ups. As such, the presence of the Yan Nian Star is useful for maintaining harmony.

If you are employed in public relations or marketing and you must interact with clients and customers as part of your daily routine, you will find the Qi brought about by this Star very useful to your career.

Do note that if the Yan Nian sector is missing, harmony and unity will be adversely affected, and relations are likely to be tense or strained. At the very least, you can expect more argument and discord with others.

West
西 (262.6°-277.5°)

Stability
伏位 (Fu Wei)

The basic characteristics of the Fu Wei Star:

It is a Star that promotes calm and keeps you grounded. It allows for peace of mind and rationality. It also promotes good luck.

The Fu Wei Star represents the Wood Element. When qualities or virtues such as calmness and tranquility are required, this is the Star you need! It promotes peace of mind and heightens clarity of thought, so this is also the Star to use if you need to focus, study or make important decisions.

If you wish to practice mediation or undertake religious and spiritual observances, the Fu Wei Star will provide the energies needed for calm and serenity, enhancing mental health and wellbeing.

This Star is most suitably applied to libraries, study areas/zones or other places where concentration is necessary. When considering the home or workplace, this Star can help create areas where the mind can be easily quietened and people can reflect and turn inward.

When the Fu Wei sector is missing from a place, peace of mind will be difficult to attain.

Unfavorable Directions

North
北 (352.6°-7.5°)

Mishaps
祸害 (Huo Hai)

The basic characteristics of the Huo Hai Star: It denotes potential calamities, accidents, and mishaps. It undermines good efforts and brings about the risk of mistakes and errors.

The Huo Hai Star represents the Earth Element and is the harbinger of mishaps, loss of wealth, sudden (unfortunate) changes or hassles as well as work-related obstacles. What it does is undermine your efforts and bring about sudden obstructions or problems that will result in a loss of time and energy.

If, for example, the Main Door of a property is located in this direction, you can reasonably expect to encounter quite a few obstacles and problems in your daily life. It is best to work around this area particularly if your main door or office is located in the West sector.

The detrimental effects of a negative star are compounded when it is located within an area that is already affected by negative Feng Shui, so pay attention to the negative structures outside this area.

South
南 (172.6°-187.5°)

Five Ghosts
五鬼 (Wu Gui)

The basic characteristics of the Wu Gui Star:

It brings about betrayal and treachery through back-stabbing, gossip, and rumors. It also denotes endless bickering and fraught tension brought about by arguments.

The Wu Gui Star represents the Fire Element and is the bringer of betrayal, ill-intentioned gossip, rumours, backstabbing, cruelty, petty people and even subterfuge and sabotage. It generally denotes a sense of unease brought upon by less-than-honest speech.

The presence of Wu Gui in a house causes disloyalty and discord amongst family members, affecting relationships and marriages. If it is present in your work place, then you should also watch out for fights and arguments between your colleagues or subordinates and friction or tension with your superiors.

Negative external forms such as (sharp) pylons and jagged rooftops pointing towards a house further aggravate the effects of this Star.

Southeast
東南 (127.6°-142.5°)

Six Killings
六煞 (Liu Sha)

The basic characteristics of the Liu Sha Star:

This Star brings about injuries and accidents. It also denotes the possibility of betrayals and dishonesty, and the risk of potential scandals.

The Liu Sha Star relates to the element of Water and is the harbinger of lawsuits and potential scandals. Legal problems at the workplace or adulterous affairs in relation to your marriage or personal relationships could be brought to light.

This Star is also the harbinger of bodily injury, harm and conditions requiring people to undergo physical surgery. Robberies and theft are also likely, and you will have to be careful about what information you share with others and with the general safety of your personal documents and possessions.

Be mindful of the presence of negative external forms, which will compound the adverse effects of this Star. For instance, a Y-shaped road at the Liu Sha sector will result in scandalous affairs, while negative structures as mentioned earlier will compound and exacerbate the harmful effects of the Liu Sha Star.

East
東 (82.6°-97.5°)

Life Threatening
絕命 *(Jue Ming)*

The basic characteristics of the Jue Ming Star:

It brings about the risk of accidents and major illness, and the threat of miscarriage for pregnant women. It also signals potential for great calamity.

This Star represents the Metal Element and it signifies accidents and illnesses. The energies of the Jue Ming Star are quite severe and so are its adverse effects, bringing with it considerable risk.

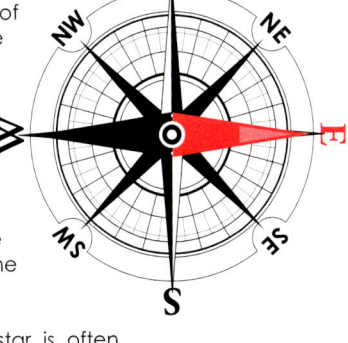

In severe cases, the Jue Ming Star can even cause fatal accidents, ailments or injuries when there are negative external forms outside of the East sector.

It is to no surprise that this star is often regarded as the primary star of misfortune and calamity in the study of Ba Zhai Feng Shui. Other than catastrophes and accidents, it can also cause major loss of wealth and theft as well as the cause of breakups or separation in relationships.

Bed Alignment Direction

One of the key Feng Shui factors of the bedroom is how your bed is placed. For starters, your bed should preferably be pushed against a wall, with the headboard also against it. The most important thing you can do when laying out your bedroom with regards to Feng Shui is to make sure your headboard is aligned with your Favorable Direction.

Facing Direction, in the case of bed alignment, refers to the direction of your headboard. This means it is the direction your head faces when you lie down on the bed, and **not** the direction that your feet face.

As a Star 7, your Bed Alignment Directions are:

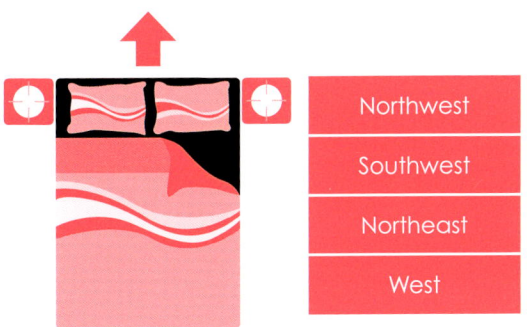

Northwest

Southwest

Northeast

West

Best Floor

A reality of modern life is that most of us do not live in houses these days, instead living in multi story apartments and condominium blocks.

Some of us are pretty mobile and live a nomad-like lifestyle that may require us to stay in high-rise buildings for certain periods of time. As such, it becomes important to select the right floor to reside in. The objective of this is to achieve elemental affinity between you (the occupant) with the energies of a particular floor.

As you are a Star 7 person of the Metal element, the chart below gives you the best floors for you to live on in terms of first choice, second choice, and third choice.

First Choice	Second Choice	Third Choice
4th Floor	5th Floor	3rd Floor
9th Floor	10th Floor	8th Floor
14th Floor	15th Floor	13th Floor
19th Floor	20th Floor	18th Floor
24th Floor	25th Floor	23rd Floor
29th Floor	30th Floor	28th Floor
34th Floor	35th Floor	33th Floor
39th Floor	40th Floor	38th Floor
44th Floor	45th Floor	43rd Floor
49th Floor	50th Floor	48th Floor

Select :
Earth shaped buildings & Metal shaped buildings

Avoid :
Fire shaped buildings & Water shaped buildings

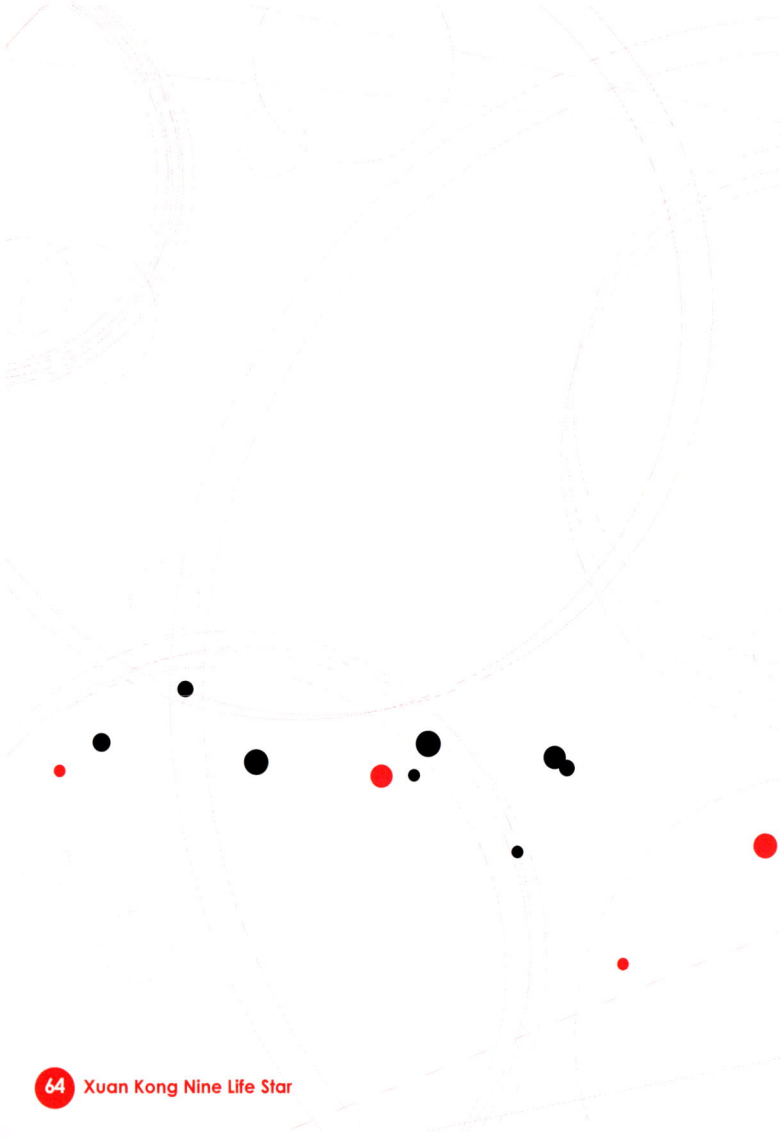

Personal Grand Duke Directions

Identifying the Grand Duke Sector is important. Your Personal Grand Duke Sector relates to your birth year. For example, if you are born in the year of the Rat then the Rat is your Personal Grand Duke and we know that the Rat sector is North 2.

We want to avoid the harmful properties of this area and as you are a Star 7 person, you can locate your Personal Grand Duke Sector in the following directions:

Personal Grand Duke Directions for Male

MALE Birth Year	Personal Grand Duke	Direction
1912, 1948, 1984, 2020	子 Zi Rat	北2 North 2
1921, 1957, 1993, 2029	酉 You Rooster	西2 West 2
1930, 1966, 2002, 2038	午 Wu Horse	南2 South 2
1939, 1975, 2011, 2047	卯 Mao Rabbit	東2 East 2

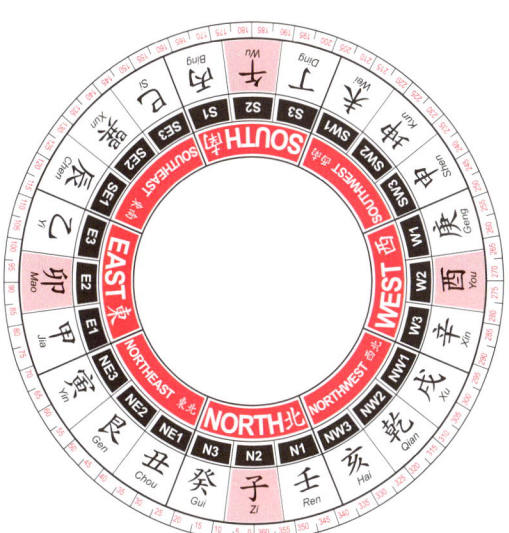

Personal Grand Duke Directions for Female

FEMALE Birth Year	Personal Grand Duke	Direction
1920, 1956, 1992, 2028	申 Shen Monkey	西南3 Southwest 3
1929, 1965, 2001, 2037	巳 Si Snake	東南3 Southeast 3
1938, 1974, 2010, 2046	寅 Yin Tiger	東北3 Northeast 3
1947, 1983, 2019, 2055	亥 Hai Pig	西北3 Northwest 3

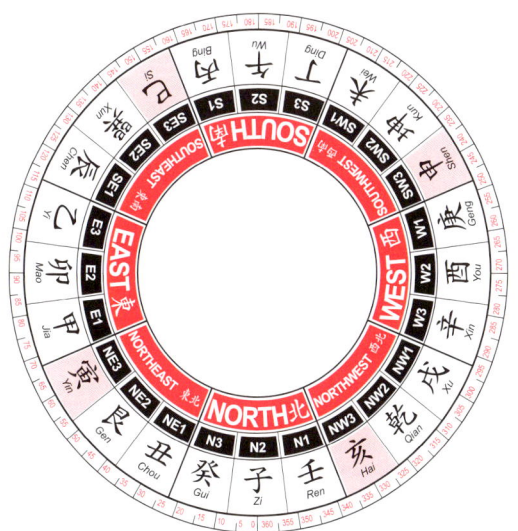

Ideally, you should not have a bathroom or toilet located in these areas of your home above and Sha Qi external features such as pylons, T-junctions, Dead Tree should be avoided. The Sha Qi in the Personal Grand Duke Sector is extremely strong and so all efforts to avoid spending a lot of time in it should be made. It goes without saying that the Personal Grand Duke Sector of your home is not the ideal spot for a bedroom! The Sha Qi in this area of the home is so strong in fact that it is difficult for any further negative Qi to enter!

Personal Clash Directions

Your home will contain Personal Clash Sectors. Spending time in these areas of your home will bring up problems in your life with significant others. As a Star 7 person, you will find your Personal Clash Sectors in the following directions:

Personal Clash Directions for Male

MALE Birth Year	Personal Clash Sector	Direction
1912, 1948, 1984, 2020	午 Wu Horse	南2 South 2
1921, 1957, 1993, 2029	卯 Mao Rabbit	東2 East 2
1930, 1966, 2002, 2038	子 Zi Rat	北2 North 2
1939, 1975, 2011, 2047	酉 You Rooster	西2 West 2

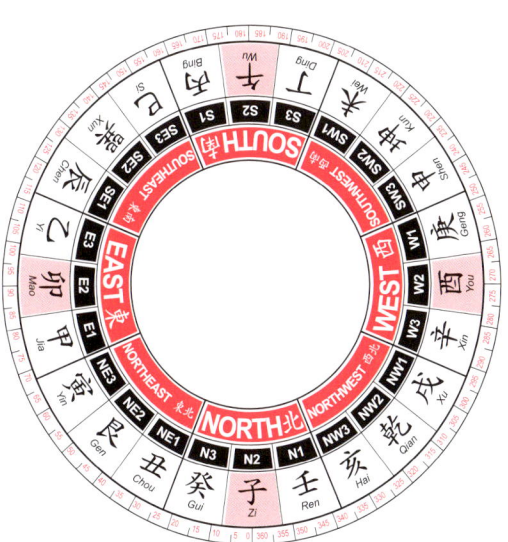

Personal Clash Directions for Female

FEMALE Birth Year	Personal Grand Duke	Direction
1920, 1956, 1992, 2028	寅 *Yin* Tiger	東北 3 Northeast 3
1929, 1965, 2001, 2037	亥 *Hai* Pig	西北 3 Northwest 3
1938, 1974, 2010, 2046	申 *Shen* Monkey	西南 3 Southwest 3
1947, 1983, 2019, 2055	巳 *Si* Snake	東南 3 Southeast 3

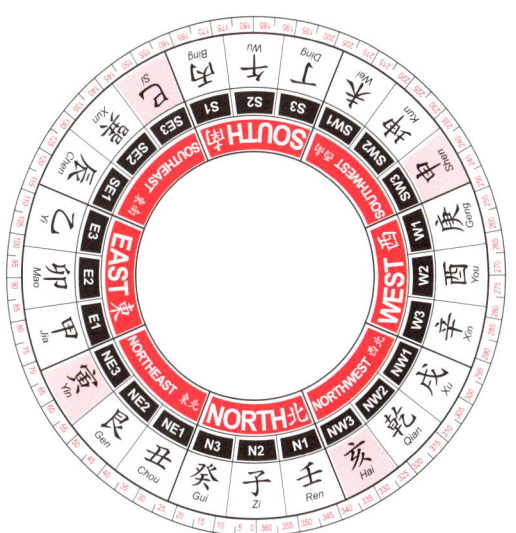

The locations above are a bad place for important features of your home such as the main door, bedroom and kitchen. You should seek to avoid these sectors in the same way you avoid your Personal Grand Duke Sector.

Flying Stars Effects

Each year, the Xuan Kong Flying Stars fly into a different section of a property, be it your residence or your work space. The effects that these Nine Stars have on you will be different depending on your Life Star. In this section you can find out how different Flying Stars in different sectors will effect you with regards to Feng Shui.

The Flying Stars have both negative and positive attributes, but which facets will show when you see a particular Star, depends on the timeliness and the period.

A few of the Nine Stars are inherently negative, a few are inherently positive in nature and some can be both good and bad. Even then, we must remember that the Stars have the capacity to manifest either their positive or negative facets because in Feng Shui, nothing is ever inherently bad or good forever.

When it comes to Flying Stars, it is important to remember this key principle: Forms activate the Stars and the Stars in turn influence the People. This is what you should keep in mind as you read about the effects of the Nine Stars on your Life Star.

1 ★ → 7 Red Life

The effects of the visiting **#1 White Star** on a **7 Red Life:**

In terms of Feng Shui effects, the presence of the #1 White is good for your career and professional ambitions, particularly if your work requires you to travel. New lucrative career advancing chances will arise and moving about will help you encounter more of these. The #1 White is also good for you as far as romance is concerned. In fact, it will seem as though matters of the heart are completely out of your hands, the way romantic opportunities seem to fall into your lap! However, bear in mind that this is also true if you're married – in which case it will be important to guard against succumbing to temptation and engaging in an affair.

2★ → 7 Red Life

The effects of the visiting **#2 Black Star** on a **7 Red Life:**

In terms of Feng Shui effects, the #2 Black creates a combination known in classical Chinese Feng Shui as 'Fire in the Early Heaven Ba Gua'. This is not a particularly auspicious Star for you, particularly if you're trying to conceive children, as the Star in particular does not bode well for women. Women living under the effects of this Star will also have to deal with some personal problems, especially if you live with your mother or daughter-in-law. There will be frequent fights and arguments that will disrupt the peace and harmony of the home.

3★ → 7 Red Life

The effects of the visiting **#3 Jade Star** on a **7 Red Life:**

In terms of Feng Shui effects, the #3 Jade will bring about the heightened risk of robbery and theft. You will have to be careful with your personal documents and perhaps increase the standard of security in your personal space. Be sure not to be careless with your belongings if there is work being done to your house. The #3 Jade also increase the odds that you will experience financial loss, probably as the result of a lawsuit. To guard yourself from this, you need to pay attention to legal documentation and make sure you comprehend all the agreements that you sign, or you could end up in a sticky mess. Watch out for eye-related illness or injuries that might occur as a result of this Star, too.

4★ → 7 Red Life

The effects of the visiting **#4 Green Star** on a **7 Red Life**:

In terms of Feng Shui effects, the presence of the #4 Green will bode very well for you, especially if you intend to travel. You will find opportunities to network and meet new people, and you may come across chances for you to explore new career trajectories or advance along your current one. However, the #4 Green increases the likelihood of respiratory illness. If you find yourself with a persistent cough, don't write it off – get it checked out. You must also be aware of the the increased risk of lawsuits or legal troubles that #4 Green brings you. Ensure that everything you engage in is above-board and sound to protect yourself from this risk.

5★ → 7 Red Life

The effects of the visiting #5 Yellow Star on a 7 Red Life:

In terms of Feng Shui effects, the presence of the #5 Yellow brings about plenty of discontent amidst relationships, which means that fights may become a frequent feature of your interactions with others. These fights tend to be triggered by bickering and backstabbing so the capacity to be hurt or taken aback is strong with the presence of the #5 Yellow. It will be very hard for you to gain peace of mind. General mental unease and varying emotions will cause you to feel disgruntled and out-of-sorts. Furthermore, you are also likely to experience possible health problems.

6★ → 7 Red Life

The effects of the visiting #6 White Star on a 7 Red Life:

In terms of Feng Shui effects, the presence of the #6 White brings about strong Metal energy. This can have negative repercussions for you as the overwhelming strength of Metal does not bode well for communication and relationships. Arguments will be common as the Star makes people hot-headed and unwilling to back down from their stance. Tension and jealousy will arise.

Furthermore, in terms of your physical health, you may be afflicted by dermatological issues.

7★ → 7 Red Life

The effects of the visiting #7 Red Star on a 7 Red Life:

In terms of Feng Shui effects, the presence of the #7 Star is quite auspicious for your wealth luck. Star 7 people should get ready to accumulate quite a bit of wealth if they capitalize on the influence of #7 Star with positive Feng Shui structures outside this sector. If there are negative structures outside this sector, be prepared for the risk of robbery and theft. Furthermore, negative structures do not bode well for you if you are Star 7 man. You could easily be tempted by charming members of the opposite sex. If you're married, you should be extra careful, as dalliances are possible. Bear in mind also that someone who sweet talks you may have an ulterior motive.

8★ → 7 Red Life

The effects of the visiting **#8 White Star** on a **7 Red Life:**

In terms of Feng Shui effects, the presence of the #8 White is good for your wealth and romantic outlook. Where money is concerned, the potential for windfall gains are likely, so you must be quick on your feet if you are to capitalizing on timely financial opportunities. This is especially true if you wish to acquire a secondary income or make good use of indirect wealth luck. The #8 White also bodes well for your romantic endeavors. Where romance is concerned, you can also use the good energies of the #8 White to meet more people and embark on a relationship if you're single. The likelihood of meeting a suitable partner is high.

9 ★ → 7 Red Life

The effects of the visiting **#9 Purple Star** on a **7 Red Life:**

In terms of Feng Shui effects, the presence of the #9 Purple can bring about problems or illness involving the heart. As such, Star 7 people of a certain age need to take greater care and exercise more caution in their daily activities. The #9 Purple also serves as a fire hazard, especially if there are external negative Feng Shui factors. In terms of personal relations, this Star brings about miscommunication, arising from bad moods and stormy temperaments. It can contribute to relationship problems.

五行

THE FIVE ELEMENTS

The Five Elements

The element of your Life Star 7 is (Yin) Metal, and it is important that you understand the implications of this. In the study of Chinese Metaphysics and Feng Shui, a basic understanding of the Five Elements is integral to success. This section will briefly outline the role of the Five Elements.

The Five Elements are symbolic representations of energy, or Qi. In Feng Shui and in BaZi, the Five Elements are Earth, Metal, Water, Wood, and Fire. Metal represents justice and fairness, and Yin Metal in particular is associated with fine metal and thus represents beauty, culture, and elegance.

In order to understand the elements, it's important to understand their relationship to one another. Each element does not exist in isolation. As such, these elements share three important relationships known as 'cycles' that are fundamental to the understanding of Feng Shui: the Productive Cycle, the Controlling Cycle, and the Weakening Cycle.

Productive Cycle

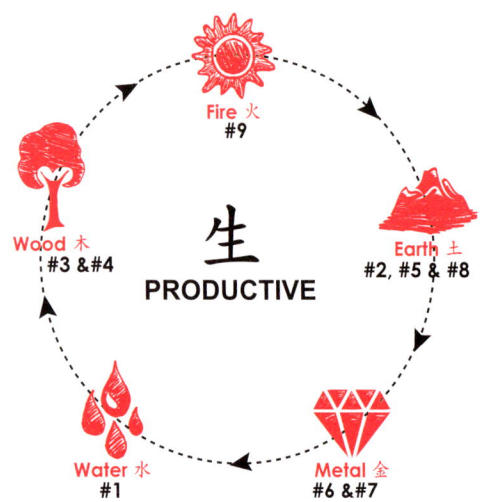

In this cycle,

Water produces Wood
Wood produces Fire
Fire produces Earth
Earth produces Metal
Metal produces Water

This is a cycle where the elements "produce" one another in terms of providing or helping the growth of another. In the case of Water, then, it produces nourishment for trees and plants (i.e. Wood). An element that produces another element means that it strengthens and grows the element that it produces. Here are some simple metaphors might help you visualize this better:

Water waters soil, producing Wood
Wood makes kindling, producing Fire
Fire makes ashes, producing Earth
Earth is mined, producing Metal
Metal melts, producing Water

Controlling Cycle

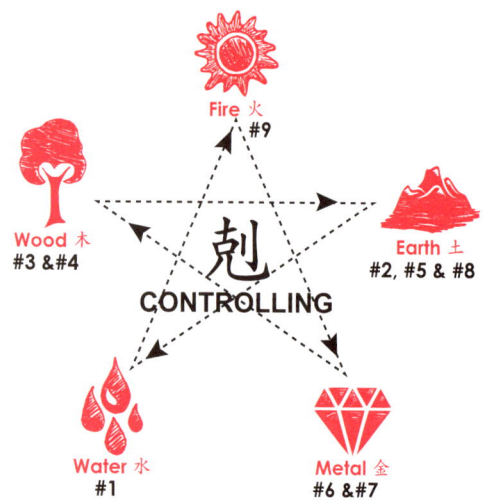

In this cycle,

Fire controls Metal
Metal controls Wood
Wood controls Earth
Earth controls Water
Water controls Fire

This is a cycle where the elements keep each under in "control": an element is countered or subjugated by its controlling element. In this instance, for example, the element of Water controls Fire by putting it out. Here are some simple metaphors to help you visualize it better:

Water extinguishes Fire
Fire melts Metal
Metal cuts Wood
Wood roots tightly grip Earth
Earth contains Water

Weakening Cycle

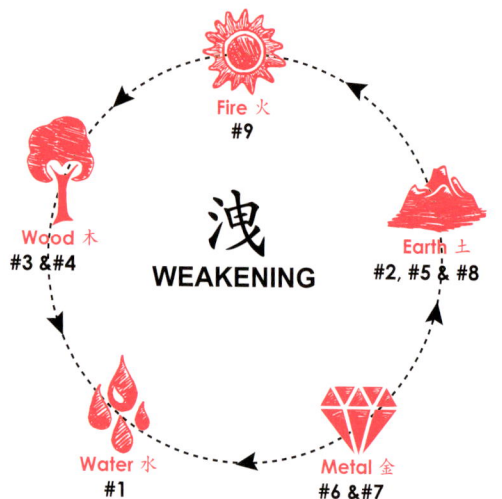

In this cycle,

Water weakens Metal
Metal weakens Earth
Earth weakens Fire
Fire weakens Wood
Wood weakens Water

The Weakening Cycle can be best understood as the reverse of the Productive Cycle, in that the strength of the element is weakened by another in order to keep it in check. Remember, the key to Qi in Feng Shui is balance, and different elements keep other elements from becoming too strong. For example, Wood absorbs Water and therefore weakens it. Again, here are some metaphors for easier visualization:

Water can be partly absorbed by Wood
Wood can be partly burnt by Fire
Fire can be diminished with Earth
Earth is weakened when mined for Metal
Metal is corroded by Water

The following table shows you the Annual Stars for the year 2000 to 2026.

Examine it and figure out where your room lies; in which sector. Take note of the element of that sector and remember that as a Star 7 person, your element is Metal.

2002, 2011, 2020

巽 SE Xun	離 S Li	坤 SW Kun
6 White METAL	2 Black EARTH	4 Green WOOD
5 Yellow EARTH	7 Red METAL	9 Purple FIRE
1 White WATER	3 Jade WOOD	8 White EARTH
艮 NE Gen	坎 N Kan	乾 NW Qian

2003, 2012, 2021

巽 SE Xun	離 S Li	坤 SW Kun
5 Yellow EARTH	1 White WATER	3 Jade WOOD
4 Green WOOD	6 White METAL	8 White EARTH
9 Purple FIRE	2 Black EARTH	7 Red METAL
艮 NE Gen	坎 N Kan	乾 NW Qian

2004, 2013, 2022

巽 SE Xun	離 S Li	坤 SW Kun
4 Green WOOD	9 Purple FIRE	2 Black EARTH
3 Jade WOOD	5 Yellow EARTH	7 Red METAL
8 White EARTH	1 White WATER	6 White METAL
艮 NE Gen	坎 N Kan	乾 NW Qian

2005, 2014, 2023

巽 SE Xun	離 S Li	坤 SW Kun
3 Jade WOOD	8 White EARTH	1 White WATER
2 Black EARTH	4 Green WOOD	6 White METAL
7 Red METAL	9 Purple FIRE	5 Yellow EARTH
艮 NE Gen	坎 N Kan	乾 NW Qian

2006, 2015, 2024

巽 SE Xun	離 S Li	坤 SW Kun
2 Black EARTH	7 Red METAL	9 Purple FIRE
1 White WATER	3 Jade WOOD	5 Yellow EARTH
6 White METAL	8 White EARTH	4 Green WOOD
艮 NE Gen	坎 N Kan	乾 NW Qian

2007, 2016, 2025

巽 SE Xun	離 S Li	坤 SW Kun
1 White WATER	6 White METAL	8 White EARTH
9 Purple FIRE	2 Black EARTH	4 Green WOOD
5 Yellow EARTH	7 Red METAL	3 Jade WOOD
艮 NE Gen	坎 N Kan	乾 NW Qian

2008, 2017, 2026

巽 SE Xun	離 S Li	坤 SW Kun
9 Purple FIRE	5 Yellow EARTH	7 Red METAL
8 White EARTH	1 White WATER	3 Jade WOOD
4 Green WOOD	6 White METAL	2 Black EARTH
艮 NE Gen	坎 N Kan	乾 NW Qian

2000, 2009, 2018

巽 SE Xun	離 S Li	坤 SW Kun
8 White EARTH	4 Green WOOD	6 White METAL
7 Red METAL	9 Purple FIRE	2 Black EARTH
3 Jade WOOD	5 Yellow EARTH	1 White WATER
艮 NE Gen	坎 N Kan	乾 NW Qian

2001, 2010, 2019

巽 SE Xun	離 S Li	坤 SW Kun
7 Red METAL	3 Jade WOOD	5 Yellow EARTH
6 White METAL	8 White EARTH	1 White WATER
2 Black EARTH	4 Green WOOD	9 Purple FIRE
艮 NE Gen	坎 N Kan	乾 NW Qian

These Annual Stars shows you the location of the Stars in a property for the duration of the years specified. Based on the year, the Annual Stars will be located in different sectors of the house. Accordingly, different Annual Stars will affect the Feng Shui of your room in different years.

If the Annual Star of your bedroom is of the same element as your Life Star then the outcome is likely to be prosperous (Productive Cycle). If the Annual Star is your Life Star's controlling element (Controlling Cycle), then the result is likely to be stressful – although this combination is still desirable. But if the Annual Star element is the countering element (Countering Cycle) of your Life Star, then the combination is an unfavorable or inauspicious one for you. (Special note: the #5 Yellow Star is generally an undesirable Annual Star for your bedroom regardless of your Life Star.)

Think about the way the element of the Annual Star and your element (Metal) interact.

Besides the Annual Stars of the year, there also other factors to be considered. These include the Flying Stars chart of your specific house or property with the Sitting and Facing Stars. Advanced students may want to read *Xuan Kong Flying Stars Feng Shui* for further information. These Stars also affect the evaluation of the impact of the Xuan Kong Flying Stars on your property. There are many other ways of assessing the Feng Shui of a property, and it's important to understand that all these factors play an important and related role.

Characteristics of Star 7

We all have our "good days" and "bad days". Feng Shui seeks to help isolate why this happens and provide advice that you can use to make every day a "good day" where you are in your element. This section outlines the good and bad characteristics of your Life Star. In a positive sector of your house or work, the positive attributes of your Life Star will be further enhanced, and you will display more of these characteristics. In a negative sector, the positive attributes will be diminished and the negative attributes will begin to show through. Your bad characteristics will take center stage.

The Good

Communicative

Out of all the Life Stars, Star 7 people possess the best verbal skills or "gift of gab". In this sense, you are very good at articulating your emotions and feelings and are known for being loquacious. This makes you communicative and engaging, and others find your chatty demeanor to be attractive. You can be described as approachable. This means that you tend to be the light which draws the moths in, and more often than not the average Star 7 character is a very popular one.

Vivacious

The Star 7 character is an energetic, cheerful, and vivacious one. Others tend to see you as spirited and full of life, and you usually exude goodwill and good energy. You can be bubbly and keeping others entertained for long periods of time is no problem for you. This is mostly because you enjoy the attention and like having people focus on you!

Resourceful

As a Star 7 person, you're also quite adept at harnessing the information, tools, and resources needed to get something done. You often have good ideas on how to start something, and you are usually the person other people turn to when they want to know how to make changes to an existing issue or situation. You have the ability to sniff out good information and find out how things are done – or at the very least, you have a good idea of where to go in order to learn these things.

Observant

Although you seem very cheerful and laid back, behind your superficial exterior lies an active mind that is constantly working. As such, you tend to be very observant and often know more than you let on, or more than people assume you do. You pay close attention to how others interact and to your surroundings in order to pick up clues on how to modify your behavior or proceed with your actions for the best outcome.

壞

The Bad

Narcissistic

One of the most pressing flaws of a Star 7 personality is your tendency to become selfish, self-absorbed, and vain. This is because you're someone who enjoys a lot of attention and thrives under the spotlight and in the gaze of admiring eyes. In the long run, however, this can mean that you become too reliant on attention and praise. As such, when in an unhealthy state, you can become overly egotistical and much too invested in yourself, your goals and your problems to the point where you stop paying attention to others entirely.

Arrogant

Because you tend to view yourself as slightly special or extraordinary, and others usually respond in kind, you tend to set a very high benchmark for how you view other people. In an unhealthy state, this can lead you to become snobbish and condescending, and if these views are left unchallenged you can slip into a state of arrogance. You may tend to assume that only what you do, say, or think is right, and will start condescending to others if they don't fit your idea of what is proper or admirable.

Materialistic

You enjoy the good life, and have a definite taste for luxury. This in itself is not a bad thing, but your desire can turn into an overwhelming obsession for more money, wealth, and beautiful things. You may start to place too much of an emphasis on 'the good life' to the point where all your actions are motivated by the need to live a good material life instead of a well rounded personal one. This can make you superficial and greedy.

Possessive

At your best, you are confident and sure of your place in the world. However, when you're not at your best, you are afraid of losing other people's attention and focus. You tend to want all the attention to be on yourself. Thus, in your personal relationships, you can become possessive, vindictive or jealous if you sense that someone is trying to 'usurp' your place at the top.

職業和財富

CAREER AND WEALTH

Characteristics at Work

As a Star 7 person, you may display some of these basic characteristics in professional situations at the workplace and in relation to your career. Being aware of your own key characteristics will help you understand why you act and react to situations, people, and tasks in the way you do.

This section outlines the good and bad characteristics of your Life Star. In a positive sector of your house or work, the positive attributes of your Life Star will be further enhanced, and you will display more of these characteristics. In a negative sector, the positive attributes will be diminished and the negative attributes will begin to show through. Your bad characteristics will take center stage.

- ### Easy-going

You tend to have a very cheerful nature regardless of where you are or who you are with and this turns out to be your hidden weapon at the workplace. Being amiable and easy-going means that others respond well to you, and your energy also renders you attractive and charismatic. In the long run, Star 7 personalities tend to be promoted up the ranks fairly quickly, as they make speedy headway with colleagues and superiors.

• Quick-witted

As a Star 7 character, you tend to possess a quick wit and great reflexes. You always give the appearance that you are on the ball and on top of everything. In a fast-paced work environment, your ability to think quickly and also improvise or adapt as necessary earns you admiration and praise from your superiors, to say nothing of the fact it generates results time and time again. These traits tend to put you in a position of leadership among everyone else.

• Motivated

You tend to perform well at work because you have a strong sense of motivation that is propelled by intense energy. You are focused and

ambitious, and don't like to lose or come in second place! As such, you are constantly inspired or even driven to find ways to reach your goals and targets, which also goes down well in the modern workplace which thrives on a KPI.

• Sociable

Many people do not appreciate just how important social skills are to progress at work but the Star 7 personality does. Utilizing people in your plans plays to your natural strengths, as you enjoy attention and like being in groups and conversing with many different people. You prove to be adept at networking and putting others at ease, be it colleagues or even clients and customers.

Suitable Job Roles

- ## Marketing, branding specialist, advertising

As a Star 7 person, you are well suited to roles in the marketing, branding, or even advertising trades because you're a natural salesperson. You can easily convince others of the merits of things that you're passionate about – particularly luxury and fine living items. A career in these fields will ask you to think on your feet, plan campaigns and socialize with a wide array of people in different fields. All of this is music to your ears!

• Life coach

Your boundless energy and can do attitude, coupled with your fondness for getting up in front of a crowd and talent for public speaking make you more than suitable for a job as a life coach or motivational trainer. A good coach takes others and inspires them to take action. Your zest for life, panache, and strong ability to express yourself and rouse enthusiasm mean that you are likely to be a natural at the job.

• Public relations, diplomat

A career in public relations or the diplomatic field will also work well for you and capitalizes on your social skills. This is because you are someone who enjoys persuading and winning

over others, and at its core, these jobs require you to win people over to your point of view. Furthermore, being clever and flexible enables you to tailor an approach to a particular subject at any given time.

• Business

Not everyone is suited for matters of business but you may have what it takes to start your own business or entrepreneurial venture...and succeed! You possess both the adaptive thinking abilities as well as the resourcefulness to make it a success. Your sense of ambition and keenness to succeed means that you will rarely attempt something without first gaining the advice and recommendations of the experts to ensure you don't fail. Starting a business is no small feat and you are meticulous enough to do it properly.

Career and Wealth Guide

• Sometimes, less is best

In money-making ventures, you can easily overreach because you can fall prey to gluttony. This is largely because you want more and dream big. You believe the only kind of life you can tolerate is the kind of life that provides you with plenty of luxury and material comforts. However, it's impossible to arrive at the standard of living you envisage in the short space of time you expect. Be ready to dig in your heels and work hard for the long term – but in the meantime, pay careful attention to small gains along the way so that you can build up confidence in your own abilities.

- # Do your research

Whether it's for starting your own business or investing your money in a new venture, ensure that you have all the information at hand before proceeding. What this means is that you need to get independent information in addition to the information you from other people, as being too reliant on other people's advice can sometimes mean you fall prey to bad advice. A little skepticism never hurts and does not have to make you a bitter person.

- ## Go deeper into yourself

As your self-perception tends to be tied to the feedback you receive from others, it will be important that you don't become complacent the moment you start receiving praise and attention. While doing well is good, and being recognized for it is better, other people's opinions are not set in stone, and are usually contingent upon something else. Don't count on public opinion as a barometer of your own success. Always strive to go beyond what you think people expect or want and define the standards of success for yourself!

• Don't focus only on success

When you label your career moves as only 'successes' or 'failures' you are likely to miss the bigger picture which tends to occur in the midst of these two extremes. Being ambitious and 'winning' something is good, but so are the moments in-between when you learn something useful or gain new experience and knowledge.

• **Forge networks**

You tend to be naturally gregarious and sociable. Use these traits your advantage at the workplace. Focus not just on making friends but on strategically utilizing your social skills in order to build alliances and contacts that can help you with your career progression. In other words, don't just socialize for fun – see it as a useful way to move ahead in your particular job role, as well

Famous Personalities :

Warren Buffett,
Roman Abramovich,
Ralph Lauren,
J.K Rowling

人際關係

RELATIONSHIPS

Guide for Relationships

As a Star 7 person, you generally will do quite well in matters of romance. Because of your bubbly, vivacious personality, others are often drawn to you because they sense you know how to have a good time and that you will show them a good time as well. You can be very polished and elegant, yet entertaining and game for fun and laughter at the drop of a hat. Star 7 women, in particular, tend to possess considerable sex appeal that turns heads.

As such, you do place priority on love and romance. In fact, once you are in a relationship, it tends to be an all-consuming affair, occupying your thoughts constantly and influencing your decisions. Because you have a rich emotional life, you can sometimes lose focus on the practical side of the relationship and become somewhat over-invested in your partner. Particularly, you require that the attention and focus of the dynamic always be on you. If this goes away, you are liable to becoming possessive, insecure, and jealous.

When you feel insecure, you have the capacity to be vindictive or somewhat cruel, although you do this out of a need to provoke a reaction. Whilst this may help you grab attention in the short term, in the long term, this will only serve to push the other person away. Step back from what you're experiencing here and now in order to evaluate the bigger picture. Make moves that benefit your long term position using short term self discipline. Empathize with your partner and consider how he/she feels about the relationship. Remember, a relationship involves two people...you are just half of the whole!

You can be choosy in selecting your partner, but this is not in itself a bad thing unless you keep eliminating potential partners based on surface appearance or image until you have no options left. Once married, however, you tend to change your perspective slightly, and become quite devoted to creating a stable home and domestic life. This is all dependent upon you finding the right partner, of course. Someone who supports you and gives you the attention you need without mollycoddling you – in other words, someone who can stand up to you! This combination in a person will earn your lasting respect.

Star 7 in relationships:

For many Star 7 people, love and romance are their number one priority. However, they sometimes ignore the practical side of relationships and may experience difficulty as a result.

健康

HEALTH

Guide for Health

Body parts and organs that are related to Star 7: Lungs, large intestine, liver, heart.

Star 7 people are generally known for having robust health, which is what contributes to your boundless energy. However, when you do fall ill, it tends to be quite serious, and ailments usually involve your lungs, lives, large intestine, gall bladder or heart.

Your digestive system is often prone to illness, too, and because you tend to enjoy a life of good living – which includes fine, luxury foods – you are at risk of overindulging on a regular basis. You need to make a conscious effort to avoid this from opening. Pay regular attention to your diet and think of small, simple changes you can make for the better and that you are likely to adhere to without sacrificing your need for a good meal and a glass of wine!

In general, it's advisable that you don't take your good health for granted, so it will be best to maintain your vitality with regular exercise. Pay more attention to your nutrition. Be careful of lung-related illnesses, or sickness that affects your mouth and respiratory system. You tend to get inflammation of the lungs, or bronchitis and coughs fairly easily. You may be frequently struck down by colds and flu if you neglect to take the proper vitamins and pay attention to your what you eat. Furthermore, keep an eye on your kidney and stomach regions, and watch out for possible skin allergies or inflammation. Consult a doctor early on if you begin developing any symptoms related to the areas mentioned above.

Potential health concerns:

Gingivitis

Toothache

Lung-related ailments

Tuberculosis (TB)

Internal bleeding or hemorrhaging

Xuan Kong Nine Life Star

COMPATIBILITY WITH OTHER LIFE STARS

This section examines your compatibility as a Star 7 person with other people who have the same and different Stars. No person goes through life completely alone. Relationships with others form the bedrock of good career networking. Friendships and relations with loved ones, spouses, partners and family make everything worth while. It is necessary to understand how compatible people with different Stars are to prevent conflict and missed opportunities. Bear in mind that issues of compatibility are not definite or set in stone. There are exceptions to every rule. In addition, **the quality of Feng Shui** in your environment helps dictate whether positive or negative traits in people manifest themselves and thus it weighs in on the quality of your relationships with those people. This section serves as a good guide on your relationships with other people of different Stars.

At a glance, Star 7 people tend to get along with fellow Metal element folks of Star 6, as there will be peace and cooperation brought about through good communication. You will also get along with fellow Star 7 people at first, but over time, there will be an element of distrust that can crop up fairly frequently,

because both Star 7 parties could end up focusing on their own needs.

You get along well with people of Star 2, 5, and 8, because these are all Earth element Stars and Earth produces Metal. Hence, these Stars can function somewhat as your Noble People in certain situations, as there will be help granted for things involving your career and wealth. The outcome with Stars 3 and 4 will also be good, as these are Wood element Stars and Metal counters Wood.

You will have to tread carefully in relationships with Star 9 people, as Fire counters Metal. As such, prospective partnerships or work relationships are likely to be the most dangerous of all. Similarly, the outcome will not necessarily be good with a Star 1 person, as it is a Water element Star and will in the long run weaken your Metal element. Any long-term, close contact partnerships will not benefit you. Avoid.

The chart below lists element people or sectors you can utilize to improve your compatibility with other Star people.

	Compatibility with others Stars (Individuals)	Seek help from this element people or use this sector
Star 7	Stars 2, 5 & 8 (Earth Element)	Fire
	Stars 3 & 4 (Wood Element)	Water
	Stars 6 & 7 (Metal Element)	Wood
	Star 9 (Fire Element)	Earth
	Star 1 (Water Element)	Metal

巽 SE Xun	離 S Li	坤 SW Kun
4 Green WOOD	**9** Purple FIRE	**2** Black EARTH
3 Jade WOOD	**5** Yellow EARTH	**7** Red METAL
8 White EARTH	**1** White WATER	**6** White METAL
艮 NE Gen	坎 N Kan	乾 NW Qian

震 E Zhen   兌 W Dui

The following pages will explain in detail the compatibility factor of a Star 7 person with people of all other nine Stars through the Compatibility Meter. The Compatibility Guides give you tips for managing the relationships in question.

| **7** Red | compatibility with | **1** White |

Compatibility Meter

When you and Star 1 person get together, the outcome depends on how you become involved with each other. On a personal level, you will probably hit it off as soon as you meet. Star 1 individuals are active and when you bring your energy and zest to the table a lot of fun can be had! They have a need to be challenged and you have an exciting and challenging approach to life! In business, however, you will end up losing out in the long run and the Star 1 person will get the upper hand. They have drive and ambition which you lack and although you are great at meeting people and making connections, they are better at manipulating others for their own needs! Star 1 individuals feel at their best when they are ahead of others and you are more concerned with attention and entertainment than you are with

the race forwards. A romantic relationship will succeed on the same merits that a friendship will but some caution is in order. When you do decide to commit you really mean it but Star 1 people are fiercely independent and are prone to stray as soon as they no longer feel fully engaged.

Compatibility Guide

When you get together with the Star 1 person, things can go smoothly but you are best advised to keep these people as friends instead of business partners. In a friendship, it will be important for you to tone down your flashiness in order not to scare off the Star 1 person. They are unlikely to complain but you may come across as self indulgent and selfish if you cannot curtain your more self centered behavior to some degree around them. Your optimism and desire to see the best in others is admirable but you must have a realistic appraisal when it comes to making romantic commitments with Star 1 individuals. You may be best advised to seek out someone who will be as loyal to you as you will be to them when the chips are down.

| **7** Red | compatibility with | **2** Black |

Compatibility Meter

When you and a Star 2 person get together, the outcome is bound to be positive.

The Star 2 person, being of the Earth element, will be useful for you in terms of career and personal advancement, as well as in guiding you towards opportunities and ventures in wealth. Your personal growth can benefit the most from Star 2 individuals. They have a natural need to nurture and care for others. It can be argued that you can be condescending or unkind to some people and that the most important person in your life is you. Although you are good at conversing with others you usually do so with you own interests in mind. Allowing a Star 2 person to show you how to think of and care for other people can enrich your world view and make you even more popular than you already are! What

goes around comes around and if you want attention and admiration from others then giving attention to their needs first is a ticket for success. Romantically, Star 2 individuals are prone to becoming submissive and dependent upon you. You may find that this suits you as you need to be the object of attention in all situations! Just don't let an unhealthy dynamic develop.

Compatibility Guide

In this connection, the impetus is on you to establish a relationship. The Star 2 person is likely to be soft hearted and introverted, and they need to be drawn out. As a highly sociable person who can show anyone how to have a good time, you are ideally suited to this task! They will greatly appreciate your talent and capabilities if you manage to take it easy and proceed to get to know them without flash and flamboyance. It will be crucial to set your ego aside so as not to intimidate them. If misunderstandings arise with the Star 2 person, they should be settled immediately or they could solidify into distance and separation.

| **7** Red | compatibility with | **3** Jade |

Compatibility Meter

When you and a Star 3 person come together, you are likely to have the upper hand.

Because Star 3 is of the Wood element, the Star 7 person of the Metal element is likely to derive greater benefits from this association. You will probably be fine with this and you will enjoy being the more important person. This is an ideal combination for both friendship and partnership, particularly if the latter involves financial trading or any sort of mutual wealth activity as together you are likely to form a winning team. You are both great with other people and confident enough to press forward. If you are entering into any kind of business partnerships, you must be aware of the rash and impulsive behavior of the Star 3 person as it can lead to bad decisions land you both in trouble. When all is said and

done, however, the basic attraction between Star 7 and Star 3 people is strong on many levels so that any conflict between you always ends in reconciliation and forgiveness. On a personal level, you will respect their impressive personality and your actions towards them will reflect this. This can form the bedrock of a relationship if you wish.

Compatibility Guide

The most important thing in dealing with the Star 3 person is to ensure that you give them space to be your equal. Being the 'dominant' party in this relationship or friendship will turn off the Star 3 person. If you hold the attitude that you are superior to them they will quickly pick up on this and any benefits you may have enjoyed from their company will not be forthcoming. It will certainly spell doom for any romantic or friendship possibilities you may have been envisaging. Keep your self importance in check. Allow them to set the pace occasionally or often to help keep them sweet.

| **7** Red | compatibility with | **4** White |

Compatibility Meter

When you and a Star 4 person come together, there is likely to be good chemistry and mutual benefits. When you meet, you can expect constant conversations that bring out both your strengths will make both of you look forward to meeting each other. Both of you will appreciate each others polished demeanor and charm. You get the admiration you crave from this person and they recognize your social prowess. If this is a business partnership, the Star 4 person will prefer that you communicate honestly and frankly about any issues that crop up as opposed to keeping silent or obfuscating the real issue. You have similar skills and are actually suited to many of the same careers which means you might well find yourself working with other Star 4 individuals. Partnership will not be without its share of hiccups and slight

power games but overall they will yield results. Romantically, Star 4 individuals enjoy cultivating drama and excitement and love itself. Your extravagant style of living is conducive to this and so romance may be likely.

Compatibility Guide

This will likely go down well if you infuse your relationship with humor, as the Star 4 person enjoys witty conversation and a good laugh. As is the case with almost all other Stars, keep your egotistical tendencies in check to avoid hurting gentle Star 4 people. At the workplace, if you do not reinforce positive messages they can become complacent, expecting others to do things for them. A well placed kind message of selfless encouragement every now and again can do wonders.

| **7** Red | compatibility with | **5** Yellow |

Compatibility Meter

The relationship between a Star 7 individual with a Star 5 individual is likely to be very good. You will probably have to take the initiative to get the relationship going as Star 5 individuals are not known for being easily approachable but once it starts it is likely to proceed well. If this is a mentorship or a work partnership, you will also find that the Star 5 person's strong input will help keep your negative traits from getting out of hand and their sensitive, compassionate side can provide you with useful knowledge you would not normally come by. You are sure to find a good way to put these people and their differing skills to use as a highly resourceful person so it is worthwhile getting to know Star 5 individuals. You may find, however, that your needs are not fully met by Star 5 people. They are highly independent and they rely only on

themselves. It is unlikely that they will shower you with the praise and admiration you have come to expect from most other people. They are also every bit as stubborn and even egotistical as you when they are in a negative state of mind. As far as romance in concerned, however, they are fiercely loyal and may make a good choice for a life partner.

Compatibility Guide

Similarly with Star 2, the impetus will be on you to drive forward the progress of the relationship, as Star 5 will be reticent to do so in relation to you. Don't let disagreements fester, as well, as this could build up to some strong resentment, and you will find it harder to address long pent-up issues when it's been going on for too long. Star 5 people have a reputation for being dull so they can definitely benefit from your sense of fun. You'll need to find a way to convince them to kick back and let their hair down once in a while!

| **7** Red | compatibility with | **6** White |

Compatibility Meter

When you and Star 6 person get together, the effect is likely to be a harmonious yet feisty relationship. Because you and the Star 6 person are of the Metal element, you will have plenty to say to each other and will never be bored. You savor exciting social situations so Star 6 individuals make ideal friends. One bone of contention may be your view of life. You are all about the here and the now – the short term fix of fun and excitement. Star 6 individuals, on the other hand, live their lives by the book. You might be tempted to break rules that they would not even dream of bending. You may find their sense of self righteousness jarring. Conversely, they may find you to be selfish or vain. There is something to be said for this, however, and that is that you may be able to teach each other to be less extreme

in your behavior and view point, encouraging mutual growth in one another. At work, this combination will probably work best when your superior is a Star 6 person because they are ideally suited to delegating tasks. You may find that they are ineffective as employees.

Compatibility Guide

This will largely be a good partnership if it involves professional or career interests. Both Star 7 and Star 6 people possess strong personalities, and hence some give-and-take is needed to avoid power struggles. On your end, you will have to give in on occasion and ignore the need to show off or to take a more dominant position, as this will only add fuel to the fire and lead to bigger arguments. Arguments will wear you out in the long run and sap you of your optimism and energy. You have to be willing to put aside your pride in the short term in order to preserve your most productive traits from being extinguished over time.

| **7** Red | compatibility with | **7** Red |

Compatibility Meter

When you get together with a Star 7 person, the result is a complex, potentially disheartening relationship. You and the Star 7 person will possess too much of similar Metal energy, and both of you will strive hard to be heard over the other. As such, while you may both be good at talking, there will be very little listening! This means that eventually cracks will begin to form. If you don't listen to one another then you will find yourselves holding no idea of what the other person is about or what they want. What could be a relationship that yields affection and results becomes little more than two people striving to show off to one another in an effort to feel good about themselves. There are limits to how long this can last. Furthermore, there will be frequent

arguments, and you will discover that the Star 7 friend is likely to be a fair-weather friend who only hangs around for the good times, and disappears during bad times. Don't expect any kind of deep connection. To look at things in a positive light, it is possible that time spent with another Star 7 individual can be like looking in a mirror. Your experience may encourage you to become more well rounded and give you an idea of how others may see you.

Compatibility Guide

If this is a friendship, it can be quite tricky, as you'll find that the other Star 7 person is quite selfish and only interested in yourselves so long as things are going well. In other words, Star 7 people are liable to be fair-weather friends to other Star 7 people. Therefore, it will be imperative for you to distinguish between the fair-weather types and the sincere types before you become too emotionally-invested in the friendship.

| **7** Red | compatibility with | **8** White |

Compatibility Meter

When Star 7 people get together with Star 8 people, the outcome is likely to be favorable for both. Star 8 people have what it takes to make good friends, but if this is a romantic relationship, it would be unrealistic to expect plain sailing. Both people will have to make significant sacrifices to accept the other before they can commit to being with each other. In the long run, however, the sacrifices may seem small as the relationship is bolstered by genuine mutual warmth and care. You might need to work a little bit to get Star 8 people to "loosen up" as they have all the ingredients of a workaholic. You can introduce a little bit of surprise and enjoyment into their lives. If you become romantically involved, the rewards are forthcoming. You just need to be patient. Star 7 people need space if they are

to articulate their feelings. In the mean time you might become frustrated at an apparent lack of reciprocal interest while they build up the courage or energy to make their feelings known. You might have to learn to wait for them to make a move in this case.

Compatibility Guide

If this is a romantic relationship, there is much love and warmth to look forward to, as loyalty and integrity are two of the foundational factors that make a relationship between a Star 7 person and a Star 8 person work. But you will have to be ready and willing to make a sacrifice, as you cannot always have things your way, and the Star 8 person may have personality quirks that you will have to work around. You must put aside one of your most dominant traits – your need to be the center of things – if you want this to work.

| **7** Red | compatibility with | **9** Purple |

Compatibility Meter

When you and a Star 9 person come together, the outcome is likely to be perilous.

The Star 9 person, being of the Fire element, may snuff out your potential enthusiasm and energy and without these key traits you are left almost powerless in everything you do. This is likely to be the case in friendships and romance. Where partnerships and business connections are concerned, however, it may be best to avoid getting into something with the Star 9 person at all, as there will likely be losses sustained by you, and potential treachery and cheating on the part of the Star 9 person. You leave yourself particularity vulnerable to this because you are unwilling to acknowledge the bad inclinations in others until it is too late.

Compatibility Guide

As this will be a tricky relationship to start with, you will have to weigh out the pros and the cons to decide if you want to proceed. This is especially true if you're embarking on either a professional partnership or a romantic relationship. There will be clear signs of personality that will establish whether or not you're willing to go forth; if you do, be prepared to weather out some storms.

About Joey Yap

Joey Yap first began learning about Chinese Metaphysics from masters in the field when he was fifteen.

Despite having graduated with a Commerce degree in Accounting, Joey never became an accountant. Instead, he began to give seminars, talks and professional Chinese Metaphysic consultations in Malaysia, Singapore, India, Australia, Canada, England, Germany and the United States, becoming a household name in the field.

By the age of twenty-six, Joey became a self-made millionaire and in 2008, he was listed in The Malaysian Tatler as the Top 300 Most Influential People in Malaysia and Prestige's Top 40 Under 40.

His practical and result-driven take on Feng Shui and BaZi sets him apart from other older, traditional masters and practitioners in the field. He shows people how the ancient teachings can be utilized for tangible REAL world benefits. The success he and his clients enjoy, thanks to his advice, is positive proof that Feng Shui and BaZi Astrology works, whether everyone believes in it or not!

Today, Joey has helped and worked with governments and the wealthiest people in Singapore, Hong Kong, China, Malaysia and Japan. His clients include multinationals, developers, tycoons and royalties. On Bloomberg, he is featured on-air as a regular guest on the subject of Feng Shui annual forecasts. He is retained by twenty-five top Malaysian property developers to help determine suitable candidates to take top management, change their space and Feng Shui mechanism, the way they make decisions, and understand the natural cosmic energies that can influence their decision-making.

Every year he conducts his 'Feng Shui and Astrology' seminar to a crowd of more than 3500 people at the Kuala Lumpur Convention Center. He also takes this annual seminar on a world tour to Frankfurt, San Francisco, New York, Las Vegas, Toronto, Sydney and Singapore.

The Joey Yap Consulting Group is the world's largest and first specialized metaphysics consultation firm. His consultancy, and professional speaking and training engagements with Microsoft, HP, Bloomberg, Citibank, HSBC and many more have seen the benefits of Classical Feng Shui and BaZi find their way into corporate environment and culture. Celebrities, property developers and other large organizations turn to Joey when they need the best.

After years of field-testing and fine-tuning his teachings, he has put together a team in the form of Joey Yap Research International. The objective of this Research Team is to scientifically track and verify the positive impact of Feng Shui and BaZi on subjects and ultimately to assist more people in achieving their life goals.

The Mastery Academy of Chinese Metaphysics which Joey founded teaches thousands of students from all around the world about Classical Feng Shui, Chinese Astrology and Face Reading. Many graduates have gone on to become successful in their own right, becoming sought after consultants, setting up their own consultancy businesses or even becoming educators, passing on Chinese Metaphysics knowledge to others.

Joey has also created the Decision Referential Technology™, offering decision reformation training on how to make better decisions in business and in personal life. He has led his team of highly trained consultants to help clients create more positive change in corporate boardrooms and increase production in their companies, helping people see their business outlook for each year so they may anticipate, plan and execute their strategies successfully.

Joey's work has been featured regularly in various popular global publications and networks like Time, Forbes, the International Herald Tribune and Bloomberg. He has also written columns for The New Straits Times, The Star and The Edge – Malaysia's leading newspapers. He has achieved bestselling author status with over sixty-five books, which have sold more than three million copies to-date.

His success is not limited to matters of Feng Shui and BaZi. Although his success is a product of them, he is also a successful entrepreneur, leading his own companies and property investment portfolio. When not teaching metaphysics or consulting around the world, Joey is a Naruto-fan, avid snowboarder and is crazy for fruits de mer.

Author's personal website :

 www.joeyyap.com

Joey Yap on Facebook:

 www.facebook.com/JoeyYapFB

MASTERY ACADEMY
OF CHINESE METAPHYSICS
Your **Preferred** Choice to the Art & Science of Classical Chinese Metaphysics Studies

Bringing **innovative** techniques
and **creative** teaching methods
to an ancient study.

Mastery Academy of Chinese Metaphysics was established by Joey Yap to play the role of disseminating this Eastern knowledge to the modern world with the belief that this valuable knowledge should be accessible to anyone, anywhere.

Its goal is to enrich people's lives through accurate, professional teaching and practice of Chinese Metaphysics knowledge globally. It is the first academic institution of its kind in the world to adopt the tradition of Western institutions of higher learning - where students are encourage to explore, question and challenge themselves and to respect different fields and branches of study - with the appreciation and respect of classical ideas and applications that have stood the test of time.

The art and science of Chinese Metaphysics studies – be it Feng Shui, BaZi (Astrology), Mian Xiang (Face Reading), ZeRi (Date Selection) or Yi Jing – is no longer a field shrouded with mystery and superstition. In light of new technology, fresher interpretations and innovative methods as well as modern teaching tools like the Internet, interactive learning, e-learning and distance learning, anyone from virtually any corner of the globe, who is keen to master these disciplines can do so with ease and confidence under the guidance and support of the Academy.

It has indeed proven to be a center of educational excellence for thousands of students from over thirty countries across the world; many of whom have moved on to practice classical Chinese Metaphysics professionally in their home countries.

At the Academy, we believe in enriching people's lives by empowering their destinies through the disciplines of Chinese Metaphysics. Learning is not an option - it's a way of life!

MASTERY ACADEMY
OF CHINESE METAPHYSICS™

MALAYSIA
19-3, The Boulevard, Mid Valley City, 59200 Kuala Lumpur, Malaysia
Tel : +603-2284 8080 | Fax : +603-2284 1218
Email   : info@masteryacademy.com
Website : www.masteryacademy.com

Australia, Austria, Canada, China, Croatia, Cyprus, Czech Republic, Denmark, France, Germany, Greece, Hungary, India, Italy, Kazakhstan, Malaysia, Netherlands (Holland), New Zealand, Philippines, Poland, Russian Federation, Singapore, Slovenia, South Africa, Switzerland, Turkey, U.S.A., Ukraine, United Kingdom

www.masteryacademy.com | +603 - 2284 8080

JOEY YAP CONSULTING GROUP

Pioneering Metaphysics - Centric Personal Coaching and Corporate Consulting

The Joey Yap Consulting Group is the world's first specialised metaphysics consultation firm. Founded in 2002 by renown international Feng Shui and BaZi consultant, author and trainer Joey Yap, the Joey Yap Consulting Group is a pioneer in the provision of metaphysics-driven coaching and consultation services for individuals and corporations.

The Group's core consultation practice areas are Feng Shui and BaZi, which are complimented by ancillary services like Date Selection, Face Reading and Yi Jing Divination. The Group's team of highly-trained professional consultants are led by Principal Consultant Joey Yap. The Joey Yap Consulting Group is the firm of choice for corporate captains, entrepreneurs, celebrities and property developers when it comes to Feng Shui and BaZi-related advisory and knowledge.

Across Industries: Our Portfolio of Clients

Our diverse portfolio of both corporate and individual clients from all around the world bears testimony to our experience and capabilities.

Joey Yap Consulting Group is the firm of choice for many of Asia's leading multi-national corporations, listed entities, conglomerates and top-tier property developers when it comes to Feng Shui and corporate BaZi.

Our services also engaged by professionals, prominent business personalities, celebrities, high-profile politicians and people from all walks of life.

JOEY YAP CONSULTING GROUP

Name (Mr./Mrs./Ms.):_____

Contact Details

Tel:_____ Fax:_____

Mobile :_____

E-mail:_____

What Type of Consultation Are You Interested In?
☐ Feng Shui   ☐ BaZi   ☐ Date Selection   ☐ Corporate Events

Please tick if applicable:
☐ Are you a Property Developer looking to engage Joey Yap Consulting Group?

☐ Are you a Property Investor looking for tailor-made packages to suit your investment requirements?

Please attach your name card here.

Thank you for completing this form. Please fax it back to us at:

Malaysia & the rest of the world
Fax : +603-2284 2213   Tel : +603-2284 1213

www.joeyyap.com

Feng Shui Consultations

For Residential Properties
- Initial Land/Property Assessment
- Residential Feng Shui Consultations
- Residential Land Selection
- End-to-End Residential Consultation

For Commercial Properties
- Initial Land/Property Assessment
- Commercial Feng Shui Consultations
- Commercial Land Selection
- End-to-End Commercial Consultation

For Property Developers
- End-to-End Consultation
- Post-Consultation Advisory Services
- Panel Feng Shui Consultant

For Property Investors
- Your Personal Feng Shui Consultant
- Tailor-Made Packages

For Memorial Parks & Burial Sites
- Yin House Feng Shui

BaZi Consultations

Personal Destiny Analysis
- Personal Destiny Analysis for Individuals
- Children's BaZi Analysis
- Family BaZi Analysis

Strategic Analysis for Corporate Organizations
- Corporate BaZi Consultations
- BaZi Analysis for Human Resource Management

Entrepreneurs & Business Owners
- BaZi Analysis for Entrepreneurs

Career Pursuits
- BaZi Career Analysis

Relationships
- Marriage and Compatibility Analysis
- Partnership Analysis

For Everyone
- Annual BaZi Forecast
- Your Personal BaZi Coach

Date Selection Consultations

- **Marriage Date Selection**
- **Caesarean Birth Date Selection**
- **House-Moving Date Selection**
- **Renovation & Groundbreaking Dates**
- **Signing of Contracts**
- **Official Openings**
- **Product Launches**

Corporate Events

Many reputable organizations and institutions have worked closely with Joey Yap Consulting Group to build a synergistic business relationship by engaging our team of consultants, led by Joey Yap, as speakers at their corporate events.

We tailor our seminars and talks to suit the anticipated or pertinent group of audience. Be it department, subsidiary, your clients or even the entire corporation, we aim to fit your requirements in delivering the intended message(s).

Tel: +603-2284 1213   Email: consultation@joeyyap.com

Chinese Metaphysics Reference Series

The Chinese Metaphysics Reference Series is a collection of reference texts, source material, and educational textbooks to be used as supplementary guides by scholars, students, researchers, teachers and practitioners of Chinese Metaphysics.

These comprehensive and structured books provide fast, easy reference to aid in the study and practice of various Chinese Metaphysics subjects including Feng Shui, BaZi, Yi Jing, Zi Wei, Liu Ren, Ze Ri, Ta Yi, Qi Men and Mian Xiang.

The Chinese Metaphysics Compendium

At over 1,000 pages, the *Chinese Metaphysics Compendium* is a unique one-volume reference book that compiles all the formulas relating to Feng Shui, BaZi (Four Pillars of Destiny), Zi Wei (Purple Star Astrology), Yi Jing (I-Ching), Qi Men (Mystical Doorways), Ze Ri (Date Selection), Mian Xiang (Face Reading) and other sources of Chinese Metaphysics.

It is presented in the form of easy-to-read tables, diagrams and reference charts, all of which are compiled into one handy book. This first-of-its-kind compendium is presented in both English and the original Chinese, so that none of the meanings and contexts of the technical terminologies are lost.

The only essential and comprehensive reference on Chinese Metaphysics, and an absolute must-have for all students, scholars, and practitioners of Chinese Metaphysics.

The Ten Thousand Year Calendar (Pocket Edition)

The Ten Thousand Year Calendar

Dong Gong Date Selection

The Date Selection Compendium

Plum Blossoms Divination Reference Book

San Yuan Dragon Gate Eight Formations Water Method

Xuan Kong Da Gua Ten Thousand Year Calendar

Bazi Hour Pillar Useful Gods - Wood

Bazi Hour Pillar Useful Gods - Fire

Bazi Hour Pillar Useful Gods - Earth

Bazi Hour Pillar Useful Gods - Metal

Bazi Hour Pillar Useful Gods - Water

Xuan Kong Da Gua Structures Reference Book

Xuan Kong Da Gua 64 Gua Transformation Analysis

Bazi Structures and Structural Useful Gods - Wood

Bazi Structures and Structural Useful Gods - Fire

Bazi Structures and Structural Useful Gods - Earth

Bazi Structures and Structural Useful Gods - Metal

Bazi Structures and Structural Useful Gods - Water

Xuan Kong Purple White Script

Earth Study Discern Truth Second Edition

www.masteryacademy.com | +603 - 2284 8080

Joey Yap's BaZi Profiling System

Three Levels of BaZi Profiling (English & Chinese versions)

In BaZi Profiling, there are three levels that reflect three different stages of a person's personal nature and character structure.

Level 1 – The Day Master

The Day Master in a nutshell is the BASIC YOU. The inborn personality. It is your essential character. It answers the basic question "WHO AM I". There are ten basic personality profiles – the TEN Day Masters – each with its unique set of personality traits, likes and dislikes.

Level 2 – The Structure

The Structure is your behavior and attitude – in other words, how you use your personality. It expands on the Day Master (Level 1). The structure reveals your natural tendencies in life – are you more controlling, more of a creator, supporter, thinker or connector? Each of the Ten Day Masters express themselves differently through the FIVE Structures. Why do we do the things we do? Why do we like the things we like? – The answers are in our BaZi STRUCTURE.

Level 3 – The Profile

The Profile reveals your unique abilities and skills, the masks that you consciously and unconsciously "put on" as you approach and navigate the world. Your Profile speaks of your ROLES in life. There are TEN roles – or Ten BaZi Profiles. Everyone plays a different role.

What makes you happy and what does success mean to you is different to somebody else. Your sense of achievement and sense of purpose in life is unique to your Profile. Your Profile will reveal your unique style.

The path of least resistance to your success and wealth can only be accessed once you get into your "flow." Your BaZi Profile reveals how you can get FLOW. It will show you your patterns in work, relationship and social settings. Being AWARE of these patterns is your first step to positive Life Transformation.

www.baziprofiling.com

BaZi Collections

Leading Chinese Astrology Master Trainer Joey Yap makes it easy to learn how to unlock your Destiny through your BaZi with these books. BaZi or Four Pillars of Destiny is an ancient Chinese science which enables individuals to understand their personality, hidden talents and abilities as well as their luck cycle, simply by examining the information contained within their birth data.

Understand and appreciate more about this astoundingly accurate ancient Chinese Metaphysical science with this BaZi Collection.

Feng Shui Collection

Must-Haves for Property Analysis!

For homeowners, those looking to build their own home or even investors who are looking to apply Feng Shui to their homes, these series of books provides valuable information from the classical Feng Shui therioes and applications.

In his trademark straight-to-the-point manner, Joey shares with you the Feng Shui do's and dont's when it comes to finding a property with favorable Feng Shui, which is condusive for home living.

Stories & Lessons on Feng Shui Series

All in all, this series is a delightful chronicle of Joey's articles, thoughts and vast experience - as a professional Feng Shui consultant and instructor - that have been purposely refined, edited and expanded upon to make for a light-hearted, interesting yet educational read. And with Feng Shui, BaZi, Mian Xiang and Yi Jing all thrown into this one dish, there's something for everyone.

www.masteryacademy.com | +603 - 2284 8080

Continue Your Journey with Joey Yap Books in Feng Shui

Pure Feng Shui
Pure Feng Shui is Joey Yap's debut with an international publisher, CICO Books, and is a refreshing and elegant look at the intricacies of Classical Feng Shui – now compiled in a useful manner for modern-day readers. This book is a comprehensive introduction to all the important precepts and techniques of Feng Shui practice.

Your Aquarium Here
This book is the first in Fengshuilogy Series, a series of matter-in-fact and useful Feng Shui books designed for the person who wants to do a fuss-free Feng Shui.

Xuan Kong Flying Stars
This book is an essential introductory book to the subject of Xuan Kong Fei Xing, a well-known and popular system of Feng Shui. Learn 'tricks of the trade' and 'trade secrets' to enhance and maximize Qi in your home or office.

Walking the Dragons
Compiled in one book for the first time from Joey Yap's Feng Shui Mastery Excursion Series, the book highlights China's extensive, vibrant history with astute observations on the Feng Shui of important sites and places. Learn the landform formations of Yin Houses (tombs and burial places), as well as mountains, temples, castles, and villages.

The Art of Date Selection: Personal Date Selection
With the *Art of Date Selection: Personal Date Selection*, learn simple, practical methods you can employ to select not just good dates, but personalized good dates. Whether it's a personal activity such as a marriage or professional endeavor such as launching a business, signing a contract or even acquiring assets, this book will show you how to pick the good dates and tailor them to suit the activity in question, as well as avoid the negative ones too!

www.masteryacademy.com | +603 - 2284 8080

Face Reading Collection

Discover Face Reding (English & Chinese versions)

This is a comprehensive book on all areas of Face Reading, covering some of the most important facial features, including the forehead, mouth, ears and even philtrum above your lips. This book eill help you analyse not just your Destiny but help you achieve your full potential and achieve life fulfillment.

Joey Yap's Art of Face Reading

The Art of Face Reading is Joey Yap's second effort with CICO Books, and takes a lighter, more practical approach to Face Reading. This book does not so much focus on the individual features as it does on reading the entire face. It is about identifying common personality types and characters.

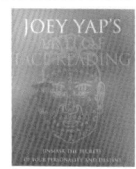

Easy Guide on Face Reading (English & Chinese versions)

The Face Reading Essentials series of books comprises 5 individual books on the key features of the face – Eyes, Eyebrows, Ears, Nose, and Mouth. Each book provides a detailed illustration and a simple yet descriptive explanation on the individual types of the features.

The books are equally useful and effective for beginners, enthusiasts, and the curious. The series is designed to enable people who are new to Face Reading to make the most of first impressions and learn to apply Face Reading skills to understand the personality and character of friends, family, co-workers, and even business associates.

Annual Releases
2011 Annual Outlook & Tong Shu

| Chinese Astrology for 2011 | Feng Shui for 2011 | Tong Shu Desktop Calendar 2011 | Professional Tong Shu Diary 2011 | Tong Shu Monthly Planner 2011 | Weekly Tong Shu Diary 2011 |

Educational Tools and Software

Xuan Kong Flying Stars Feng Shui Software
The Essential Application for Enthusiasts and Professionals

The Xuan Kong Flying Stars Feng Shui Software will assist you in the practice of Xuan Kong Feng Shui with minimum fuss and maximum effectiveness. Superimpose the Flying Stars charts over your house plans (or those of your clients) to clearly demarcate the 9 Palaces. Use it to help you create fast and sophisticated chart drawings and presentations, as well as to assist professional practitioners in the report-writing process before presenting the final reports for your clients. Students can use it to practice their Xuan Kong Feng Shui skills and knowledge, and it can even be used by designers and architects!

BaZi Ming Pan Software Version 2.0
Professional Four Pillars Calculator for Destiny Analysis

The BaZi Ming Pan Version 2.0 Professional Four Pillars Calculator for Destiny Analysis is the most technically advanced software of its kind in the world today. It allows even those without any knowledge of BaZi to generate their own BaZi Charts, and provides virtually every detail required to undertake a comprehensive Destiny Analysis.

This Professional Four Pillars Calculator allows you to even undertake a day-to-day analysis of your Destiny. What's more, all BaZi Charts generated by this software are fully printable and configurable! Designed for both enthusiasts and professional practitioners, this state-of-the-art software blends details with simplicity, and is capable of generating 4 different types of BaZi charts: **BaZi Professional Charts, BaZi Annual Analysis Charts, BaZi Pillar Analysis Charts and BaZi Family Relationship Charts.**

Joey Yap Feng Shui Template Set

Directions are the cornerstone of any successful Feng Shui audit or application. The **Joey Yap Feng Shui Template Set** is a set of three templates to simplify the process of taking directions and determining locations and positions, whether it's for a building, a house, or an open area such as a plot of land, all with just a floor plan or area map.

The Set comprises 3 basic templates: The Basic Feng Shui Template, 8 Mansions Feng Shui Template, and the Flying Stars Feng Shui Template.

Mini Feng Shui Compass

The Mini Feng Shui Compass is a self-aligning compass that is not only light at 100gms but also built sturdily to ensure it will be convenient to use anywhere. The rings on the Mini Feng Shui Compass are bi-lingual and incorporate the 24 Mountain Rings that is used in your traditional Luo Pan.

The comprehensive booklet included will guide you in applying the 24 Mountain Directions on your Mini Feng Shui Compass effectively and the 8 Mansions Feng Shui to locate the most auspicious locations within your home, office and surroundings. You can also use the Mini Feng Shui Compass when measuring the direction of your property for the purpose of applying Flying Stars Feng Shui.

Educational Tools and Software

Xuan Kong Vol.1
An Advanced Feng Shui Home Study Course

Learn the Xuan Kong Flying Star Feng Shui system in just 20 lessons! Joey Yap's specialised notes and course work have been written to enable distance learning without compromising on the breadth or quality of the syllabus. Learn at your own pace with the same material students in a live class would use. The most comprehensive distance learning course on Xuan Kong Flying Star Feng Shui in the market. Xuan Kong Flying Star Vol.1 comes complete with a special binder for all your course notes.

Feng Shui for Period 8 - (DVD)

Don't miss the Feng Shui Event of the next 20 years! Catch Joey Yap LIVE and find out just what Period 8 is all about. This DVD boxed set zips you through the fundamentals of Feng Shui and the impact of this important change in the Feng Shui calendar. Joey's entertaining, conversational style walks you through the key changes that Period 8 will bring and how to tap into Wealth Qi and Good Feng Shui for the next 20 years.

Xuan Kong Flying Stars Beginners Workshop - (DVD)

Take a front row seat in Joey Yap's Xuan Kong Flying Stars workshop with this unique LIVE RECORDING of Joey Yap's Xuan Kong Flying Stars Feng Shui workshop, attended by over 500 people. This DVD program provides an effective and quick introduction of Xuan Kong Feng Shui essentials for those who are just starting out in their study of classical Feng Shui. Learn to plot your own Flying Star chart in just 3 hours. Learn 'trade secret' methods, remedies and cures for Flying Stars Feng Shui. This boxed set contains 3 DVDs and 1 workbook with notes and charts for reference.

BaZi Four Pillars of Destiny Beginners Workshop - (DVD)

Ever wondered what Destiny has in store for you? Or curious to know how you can learn more about your personality and inner talents? BaZi or Four Pillars of Destiny is an ancient Chinese science that enables us to understand a person's hidden talent, inner potential, personality, health and wealth luck from just their birth data. This specially compiled DVD set of Joey Yap's BaZi Beginners Workshop provides a thorough and comprehensive introduction to BaZi. Learn how to read your own chart and understand your own luck cycle. This boxed set contains 3 DVDs and 1 workbook with notes and reference charts.

www.masteryacademy.com | +603 - 2284 8080

DVD Series

Joey Yap's Face Reading Revealed DVD Series

Mian Xiang, the Chinese art of Face Reading, is an ancient form of physiognomy and entails the use of the face and facial characteristics to evaluate key aspects of a person's life, luck and destiny. In his Face Reading DVDs series, Joey Yap shows you how the facial features reveal a wealth of information about a person's luck, destiny and personality.

Mian Xiang also tell us the talents, quirks and personality of an individual. Do you know that just by looking at a person's face, you can ascertain his or her health, wealth, relationships and career? Let Joey Yap show you how the 12 Palaces can be utilised to reveal a person's inner talents, characteristics and much more.

Feng Shui for Homebuyers DVD Series

In these DVDs, you will also learn how to identify properties with good Feng Shui features that will help you promote a fulfilling life and achieve your full potential. Discover how to avoid properties with negative Feng Shui that can bring about detrimental effects to your health, wealth and relationships.

Joey will also elaborate on how to fix the various aspects of your home that may have an impact on the Feng Shui of your property and give pointers on how to tap into the positive energies to support your goals.

Discover Feng Shui with Joey Yap: Set of 4 DVDs
Informative and entertaining, classical Feng Shui comes alive in *Discover Feng Shui with Joey Yap!*

You have the questions. Now let Joey personally answer them in this 4-set DVD compilation! Learn how to ensure the viability of your residence or workplace, Feng Shui-wise, without having to convert it into a Chinese antiques' shop. Classical Feng Shui is about harnessing the natural power of your environment to improve quality of life. It's a systematic and subtle metaphysical science.

Walking the Dragons with Joey Yap (The TV Series)

This DVD set features eight episodes, covering various landform Feng Shui analyses and applications from Joey Yap as he and his co-hosts travel through China. It includes case studies of both modern and historical sites with a focus on Yin House (burial places) Feng Shui and the tombs of the Qing Dynasty emperors.

The series was partly filmed on-location in mainland China, and the state of Selangor, Malaysia.

www.masteryacademy.com | +603 - 2284 8080

Home Study Courses

Gain Valuable Knowledge from the Comfort of Your Home

Now, armed with your trusty computer or laptop and Internet access, knowledge of Chinese Metaphysics is just a click away!

3 easy steps to activate your Home Study Course:

Step 1:
Go to the URL as indicated on the Activation Card, and key in your Activation Code

Step 2:
At the Registration page, fill in the details accordingly to enable us to generate your Student Identification (Student ID).

Step 3:
Upon successful registration, you may begin your lessons immediately.

Joey Yap's Feng Shui Mastery HomeStudy Course

Module 1: **Empowering Your Home**
Module 2: **Master Practitioner Program**

Learn how easy it is to harness the power of the environment to promote health, wealth and prosperity in your life. The knowledge and applications of Feng Shui will no more be a mystery but a valuable tool you can master on your own.

Joey Yap's BaZi Mastery HomeStudy Course

Module 1: **Mapping Your Life**
Module 2: **Mastering Your Future**

Discover your path of least resistance to success with insights about your personality and capabilities, and what strengths you can tap on to maximize your potential for success and happiness by mastering BaZi (Chinese Astrology). This course will teach you all the essentials you need to interpret a BaZi chart and more.

Joey Yap's Mian Xiang Mastery HomeStudy Course

Module 1: **Face Reading**
Module 2: **Advanced Face Reading**

A face can reveal so much about a person. Now, you can learn the art and science of Mian Xiang (Chinese Face Reading) to understand a person's character based on his or her facial features with ease and confidence.

www.masteryacademy.com | +603 - 2284 8080

Feng Shui Mastery™
LIVE COURSES (MODULES ONE TO FOUR)

The Feng Shui Mastery™ comprises Feng Shui Mastery Modules 1, 2, 3 and 4. It starts off with a foundation program up to the advanced practitioner level. It is a thorough, comprehensive program that covers important theories from various classical Feng Shui systems including Ba Zhai, San Yuan, San He, and Xuan Kong.

Module One: Beginners Course **Module Two:** Practitioners Course **Module Three:** Advanced Practitioners Course **Module Four:** Master Course

BaZi Mastery™
LIVE COURSES (MODULES ONE TO FOUR)

The BaZi Mastery™ consists of BaZi Mastery Modules 1, 2, 3 and 4. In Modules 1 and 2, students will receive a thorough introduction to BaZi, along with an intensive understanding of BaZi principles and the requisite skills to practice it with accuracy and precision. This will prepare them, and serious Feng Shui practitioners, for a more advanced levels and fine-tune their application skills in Modules 3 and 4.

Module One: Intensive Foundation Course **Module Two:** Practitioners Course **Module Three:** Advanced Practitioners Course **Module Four:** Master Course in BaZi

Xuan Kong Mastery™
LIVE COURSES (MODULES ONE TO THREE)
* Advanced Courses For Master Practitioners

The Xuan Kong Mastery™ comprises Xuan Kong Mastery Modules 1, 2A, 2B and 3. It is a sophisticated branch of Feng Shui replete with many techniques and formulae, enabling practitioners to evaluate Feng Shui on a more thorough and in-depth basis. The study of Xuan Kong encompasses numerology, symbology and science of the Ba Gua along with the mathematics of time.

Module One: Advanced Foundation Course **Module Two A:** Advanced Xuan Kong Methodologies **Module Two B:** Purple White **Module Three:** Advanced Xuan Kong Da Gua

www.masteryacademy.com | +603 - 2284 8080

Mian Xiang Mastery™
LIVE COURSES (MODULES ONE AND TWO)

The Mian Xiang Mastery™ comprises of Mian Xiang Mastery Modules 1 and 2 to allow students to learn this ancient art in a thorough, detailed manner. Each module has a carefully-developed syllabus that allows students to get acquainted with the fundamentals of Mian Xiang before moving on to the more intricate theories and principles that will enable them to practice Mian Xiang with greater depth and complexity.

Module One: Basic Face Reading

Module Two: Practical Face Reading

Yi Jing Mastery™
LIVE COURSES (MODULES ONE AND TWO)

The Yi Jing Mastery™ comprises Modules 1 and 2. Both Modules aim to give casual and serious Yi Jing enthusiasts a serious insight into one of the most important philosophical treatises in ancient Chinese thought. Yi Jing uses sophisticated formulas and calculations to derive the answers to questions we pose. It is a science of divination, and in our classes there is a heavy emphasis on the scientific aspect of it. It bears no religious or superstitious affiliation.

Module One: Traditional Yi Jing

Module Two: Plum Blossom Numerology

Ze Ri Mastery™
LIVE COURSES (MODULES ONE AND TWO)

The ZeRi Mastery™ consists of ZeRi Mastery Modules 1 and 2. This program provides students with a thorough introduction to the art of Date Selection both for Personal and Feng Shui purposes. Our ZeRi Mastery™ aims to provide a thorough and comprehensive program on the art of Date Selection, covering everything from Personal and Feng Shui Date Selection to Xuan Kong Da Gua Date Selection.

Module One: Personal and Feng Shui Date Selection

Module Two: Xuan Kong Da Gua Date Selection

www.masteryacademy.com | +603 - 2284 8080

Feng Shui for Life

This is an entry-level five-day course designed for the Feng Shui beginner to learn the application of practical Feng Shui in day-to-day living. Lessons include quick tips on analyzing the BaZi chart, simple Feng Shui solutions for the home, basic Date Selection, useful Face Reading techniques and practical Water formulas. A great introduction course on Chinese Metaphysics studies for beginners.

Joey Yap's
Design Your Destiny

This is a three-day life transformation program designed to inspire awareness and action for you to create a better quality of life. It introduces the DRT™ (Decision Referential Technology) method, which utilizes the BaZi Personality Profiling system to determine the right version of you, and serves as a tool to help you make better decisions and achieve a better life in the least resistant way possible based on your Personality Profile Type.

Walk the Mountains! Learn Feng Shui in a Practical and Hands-on Program

Feng Shui Mastery Excursion™

Learn landform (Luan Tou) Feng Shui by walking the mountains and chasing the Dragon's vein in China. This Program takes the students in a study tour to examine notable Feng Shui landmarks, mountains, hills, valleys, ancient palaces, famous mansions, houses and tombs in China. The Excursion is a 'practical' hands-on course where students are shown to perform readings using the formulas they've learnt and to recognize and read Feng Shui Landform (Luan Tou) formations.

Read about China Excursion here:
http://www.fengshuiexcursion.com

Mastery Academy courses are conducted around the world. Find out when will Joey Yap be in your area by visiting **www.masteryacademy.com** or call our office at **+603-2284 8080**.

www.masteryacademy.com | +603 - 2284 8080